In *Transformed: The 7 Pillars of a Legacy Minded Man*, Joe Pellegrino and Jack Redmond crystalize what every responsible man should aspire to, embrace, and run with. They have written the vision and made it plain. Silence the voices seeking to eliminate manhood from culture by leaving a powerful legacy.

—GERALD BELL, DeVos Urban Leadership

Strong men of faith and character are needed now more than ever! In *Transformed*, Joe and Jack give men the needed tools to develop a winning game plan for their own life while establishing a strong legacy for other men.

—DAVID D. IRELAND, Ph.D., Lead Pastor, Christ Church, and author of *Raising a Child Who Prays*, www.DavidIreland.org

I founded the K.I.N.G. Movement to empower and encourage men to be healthy in all aspects of life. Joe and Jack's book *Transformed* is a powerful resource that can help men achieve that goal. Informative and inspiring, *Transformed* can help men break free from the invisible chains that leave them shackled in mediocrity (or worse) and jump-start them on the path toward fulfilling their destiny.

—CHRIS BROUSSARD, NBA reporter/analyst, www.KingMovement.com

For more than twenty years of my life, I lived as a "made man," a soldier and caporegime in New York's Colombo crime family. I was blessed to have been able to walk away from that life and survive some very serious challenges only a merciful and loving God could have provided for. I have since come to realize that being a "made man" was a misguided choice I once made, and that being a "Legacy Minded Man" is what I now strive to be. A legacy-minded man possesses all the qualities of character a man needs to be a real "man's man," a standard every man should want to achieve throughout his life. I can honestly say that *Transformed: The 7 Pillars of a Legacy Minded Man* is a *blueprint* for every man, providing all the qualities of character a man needs to become a real man's man. In doing so, he will leave behind a God-ordained legacy for his children, grandchildren, and everyone who will be so blessed to have come in contact with him. I highly recommend this book, guys, and this is an offer you should not refuse!

—MICHAEL FRANZESE, former New York mobster with the
Colombo crime family, inspirational speaker, and author

Calling all men! It's time to report for duty. It's time to be the man you were created to be! Joe Pellegrino and Jack Redmond are sounding the alarm to wake up men everywhere and provide them wise advice so they can fully grasp the awesome blessing of manhood.

—KELLY WRIGHT, *Fox News* anchor

Excellent book! Joe Pellegrino and Jack Redmond have set the table for a powerful move of God among men with this book. The honesty and transparency of these men are refreshing, and the insights are deep. May God help us to become men of integrity, Legacy Minded Men!

—REV. PETER AMMERMAN, Pastor, Living Waters Church

My friend, Joe Pellegrino, and Jack Redmond have written a very good book that will be a blessing to many men. We must think about our legacy, not just what we want to do this weekend. Joe and Jack help us focus on the long term, on what is really important. That is a Key Success Factor for all of us who want to be a good husband, great father, and a faithful friend. You're going to enjoy this book!

—THE HONORABLE GREGORY W. SLAYTON, author of the global
best-seller *Be a Better Dad Today: Ten Tools Every Father Needs*

Written in an engaging and down-to-earth manner, *Transformed* lays a great foundation for men to take a reality check on where they are. While we can do a lot of talking as men, this book gives you the space to reflect and then take action! If you're like me, you'll have struggled with, are struggling with, or will struggle with one or more of these areas. Read this book because there is wisdom here. You won't be disappointed. Makes for a great men's group discussion too!

—CHUCK EAPEN, President/CEO, C12 Group,
northern New Jersey

The greatest endorsement of a book like *Transformed* is whether the content actually works in real-life situations. I have been personally involved in groups utilizing the 7 Pillars material, and the results are wonderful. Lives are changed! *Transformed* is fresh and practical, and translates the truths of the biblical principles described into ways that men can grasp and implement in their own lives. If you're looking for a manual for manhood, this is the book for you!

—JOE BATTAGLIA, broadcaster, president of Renaissance
Communications, a media-marketing company, and
author of *The Politically Incorrect Jesus* and *That's My Dad!*

Transformed: The 7 Pillars of a Legacy Minded Man will help provide the tools necessary for you as a man to build a strong foundation in Christ. Joe and Jack will teach you how to prioritize your life, assuring that your legacy will impact not only those who know you personally, but also the lives of future generations. It is a must-read if you want to ensure your legacy as a disciple of Christ.

—ROB BILLINGHAM, Executive Director,
Training Camp Men's Ministries

One of the greatest needs today in our society is to help men be strong husbands and fathers. *Transformed* can help men build the character and strength needed to navigate and overcome life's challenges and come out victorious!

—MALIK M. CAREY, vice president and COO, The K.I.N.G. Movement Men's Ministry, www.KingMovement.com

TRANSFORMED

The 7 Pillars of a Legacy Minded Man

JOE PELLEGRINO
JACK REDMOND

BroadStreet
P U B L I S H I N G

BroadStreet Publishing Group, LLC
Racine, Wisconsin, USA
BroadStreetPublishing.com

Transformed: The 7 Pillars of a Legacy Minded Man

ISBN-13: 978-1-4245-5267-2 (softcover)
ISBN-13: 978-1-4245-5268-9 (e-book)

Stock or custom editions of BroadStreet Publishing titles may be purchased in bulk for educational, business, ministry, fundraising, or sales promotional use. For information, please e-mail info@broadstreetpublishing.com.

Cover design by Chris Garborg, garborgdesign.com
Interior design and typeset by Katherine Lloyd, TheDESKonline.com

Printed in the United States of America

16 17 18 19 20 5 4 3 2 1

We would like to dedicate this book to
our families, who love us,
our friends, who support us, and
our Lord, who saved us.

—*Joe and Jack*

CONTENTS

FOREWORD

The real problem with the culture in which we live today is that we all know there's a problem but very few of us are working toward a solution. Then along comes a man named Joe Pellegrino, who not only recognizes the problems but has a godly solution that can rid us of the lethargy and the lack of accountability that is so prevalent in male ministry today.

We tend to think that male problems can be solved with programs that engage a man in mostly secular semispiritual activities. But many failed attempts lead us to believe this is not an adequate solution. *Transformed: The 7 Pillars of a Legacy Minded Man* is not a book of theoretical suppositions. Rather, it actually presents seven pillars that all men who endeavor to leave a lasting legacy must establish as absolutes in their lives.

It is challenging to live without a strategy. But many men drift through life making mistakes from which they learn almost nothing, which is evidenced by the fact that they make the same mistakes over and over again. This book is designed to stop that downward spiral and give men the hope to believe they can make it to the top. Prayer, persona, purity, purpose, priority, perseverance, and power are mighty weapons that, if placed in the arsenal of a man, will guarantee his success in the attempt to win at life. I believe this is a must-read for all legacy-minded men.

—Bishop Roderick R. Caesar

FIRST A LITTLE BACKGROUND

My name is Joe Pellegrino, and I am just a regular guy, an average Joe. May 26, 1995, is my reset date. It was on that day, during a Promise Keepers conference in Washington, DC, that God offered me a do-over. And I took it, putting my life in the hands of Jesus Christ. I realized what a shameful excuse of a man I had been for the first thirty-three years of my life—there was so much sin. And I mean *so* much sin. But that all began to change the day I accepted the gift to walk with Jesus Christ. Since then, my life has been a process of growth, transformation, and, even at times, failing forward.

Before I met Christ, I had been building my life like a man building his house on the sand. My life lacked a solid foundation. That day in 1995, however, I traded the foundation of sand and replaced it with a life foundation of solid rock (Luke 6:46–49). This new start gave me a strong base upon which to build my life, which was only the beginning. I finally had the right foundation, but I still needed the rest of the house.

The internal structure, made up of pillars and beams, comes next and supports everything else. Too many men stop with the foundation of their new life in Christ. But it is important to understand that Jesus Christ didn't come just to save us from our sin; He came so that we could, through His divine power, build a new and different life in Him (John 10:10).

Just as my life before Christ lacked a solid foundation, it also had faulty pillars. A pillar supports weight, and several of them are required to hold up a structure. Up until that fateful day in DC, my pillars either didn't exist or they had crumbled under the weight of my life and my sin. My pillars were built with cheap, inferior materials. I was cutting corners and taking the easy way out in order to build my empire quickly, only to find that my handiwork was insufficient amidst the storms of life and beneath the weight of my sin.

Through many painful life experiences, I learned that I would need something stronger and more reliable than myself as a foundation to build upon, and I learned that I would need better pillars to hold things up. On that day in 1995, after thirty-three years of paying dearly for my faulty design, I began working from a better blueprint. I traded my life plans for God's. It was an awesome moment, and the journey of rebuilding began.

A Life of Lasting Impact

This book will point you toward the foundation of Jesus Christ and help you build a life on Him. It will also point you to the kinds of structures Jesus wants for your life. The foundation and pillars described will result in a life of lasting impact. In fact, they are the keys to becoming a legacy-minded man. To be clear, this is a book written by flawed men. It is not a substitute for the Bible, the book written by the Author of life Himself. Therefore, the Bible is the book to study. The book now before you, *Transformed*, is designed to help you along the journey with Him.

As the founder of Legacy Minded Men, an organization

dedicated to "transforming lives by engaging, encouraging, and equipping men to build a Christ-centered legacy," I have learned that when I take the time, make the right investment in materials, and have the right builder, it makes all the difference in the world. I've discovered seven pillars that can stand the test of life.

These seven pillars are nonnegotiable skills. Men can and should master them and use them to build their life on their newfound, solid foundation. These pillars will hold up, no matter what your life looks like. And they will outlast you. You don't want to just have a good season or a good run. You want to have a good life. Your life will affect the generations to follow—that is your legacy. If you build well, what you build will stand long after you leave this world. This is the way a legacy-minded man thinks.

What Is a Man's Legacy?

leg·a·cy [leg-*uh*-see] noun, plural leg·a·cies.

1. *Law.* a gift of property, especially personal property, as money, by will; a bequest.

2. anything handed down from the past, as from an ancestor or predecessor.[1]

A legacy is a gift of property, which is usually given from an ancestor or a predecessor. But the definition could also include the skills and examples we learn from those who have gone before us. This means that a legacy-minded man lives so that he will have something valuable to hand down to his children, the next generation, the church, or to society as a whole. Some of these gifts are material, but many of them are spiritual or character based.

The reality is that we all hand down something. Some people leave treasured gifts, others leave debt. Some men leave great morals and family history, while others leave utter chaos. Some men leave a strong spiritual heritage, and others leave generational sin. The chances are you have certain possessions or character traits you are proud to hand down. And chances are even better that you have things you pray will end with you.

If that is the case, then you're just like me. Before God began His work in my life, my legacy wasn't looking good, so I made some changes. And I believe you are man enough to make changes too. If the legacy you are leaving now stinks, don't give up. Rather, have the courage to change it. Through it all, know this: you are not alone.

Yesterday Is Gone

I've failed many times in my life. I've also had many successes. Both extremes have been part of my life—the thrill of victory and the agony of defeat. The truth is, I have lived through both. While victory and success have driven me forward to do greater things, I've probably learned more from failure. That's because long ago I decided to let failure be my life coach, inviting it to teach me what I really needed to know.

Along the way, I decided I would win in life. Although my definition of winning has definitely changed over the years, I now know that the only victory is in Christ and Christ alone. I also decided to live a life that would make a difference long after I'm gone. I didn't want to be someone who lived comfortably now, but did nothing to make the world a better place. And I further decided to help other men succeed where I had failed—to teach them to be husbands and fathers in ways I wasn't.

I want to invite you to choose victory and to choose to help others win too. And I would love to help you do this. But remember, just as when the cabin in an aircraft loses pressure and the air mask drops down, the first thing you need to do is help yourself. It is only then that you can help others.

A legacy-minded man lives so that he wins, day in and day out. He honors God, he loves his wife, he trains his children, and he overcomes failure because he understands that God created him to succeed. All of this is a process, and *Transformed: The 7 Pillars of a Legacy Minded Man* is a map for the journey. You may swing and miss, but you have to get back to the plate and swing again. If you strike out, then you work, you practice, and you get coached—and then you step up to the plate again. You keep at it. When you're up in the bottom of the ninth, you hit that walk-off home run. That's what God has created you to do, and Legacy Minded Men is here to help you get there.

You Can Change

I am living proof that anyone can change. As a child, teen, and young adult, I was a chronic liar. In fact, I lied so much that I actually believed the lies I was telling, so much so that to this day I still cannot decipher some events as the product of my imagination or real events that truly happened. I also accepted the lies that society told me. Eventually, however, I learned from God's Word that the truth would set me free. So I made the choice to stop the habitual lying, stop accepting the lies of others, and, most importantly, to stop living lies.

My prayer is that through *Transformed,* God will help you win in life. These seven pillars will focus on God's Word—what He says about life and how it should be lived. We'll answer questions like:

- Why are the seven pillars crucial to building my legacy?

- What does this look like in real life?

- How do I walk this out?

- How do I build these pillars in my life?

As you read this book, you will find over seven hundred instances where the word *I* is used. Stanford University did a study that revealed that only 5 percent of their students were able to remember points made in a lecture when statistics were the foundation of the talk. But over 60 percent of the students were able to recall a lecture when an "I" story was introduced to cement the message. Therefore, we (Jack Redmond, my friend and coauthor, and I) felt led to share stories, primarily from our own lives, to illustrate each pillar presented. Some will make us look bad. We're okay with that, because we know that we have all done things we are ashamed of. But some of the stories will make us look good. We're not trying to brag; we only want to help you remember the pillars.

It's easier to build a great legacy when you are surrounded by other legacy-minded men. Join us. Our team is big and strong, growing every day. Hey, you may just be an average Joe, just like me, imperfect in so many ways, but that should not stop you from being bold and doing great things in His name and for His glory.

Paul laid out for us what it means to be a legacy-minded man in a concise manner: "Be on your guard; stand firm in the faith; be men of courage; be strong. Do everything in love" (1 Corinthians 16:13–14). That's how I have chosen to live. What about you? Remember, yesterday does not have to define you if you use today to refine you. It's up to you. Seize the moment!

—Joe Pellegrino

BUILT ON THE ROCK

The seven pillars described in this book will help you build a great life and a lasting legacy. But that will only happen if they are built on the foundation of a relationship with Jesus Christ and His Word. Simply put, it all begins with an understanding of the gospel.

What Is the Gospel?

When God created Adam, His intention was to have an intimate and unhindered relationship with him. There would be no suffering or death; there would be no evil or sin. However, God gave him free will, which enabled him to rebel against God, resulting in humanity's separation from God (Genesis 3). But God's great love for us caused Him to create a plan for our redemption, "buying us back" from the debt we owe due to our sin.

God's plan begins to take shape in Genesis 3:21, when death enters the world. Ultimately, when Jesus came, died, and rose from the dead, He once and for all paid for sin (Hebrews 9:12–14; 10:10). We are given the free gift of salvation through the death of Christ, just as the free gift of sin was given through the work of one man's sin. But as with any gift, salvation must be received. Paul writes of this in Romans 5:12–21:

Therefore, just as sin entered the world through one man, and death through sin, and in this way death came to all men, because all sinned—for before the law was given, sin was in the world. But sin is not taken into account when there is no law. Nevertheless, death reigned from the time of Adam to the time of Moses, even over those who did not sin by breaking a command, as did Adam, who was a pattern of the one to come.

But the gift is not like the trespass. For if the many died by the trespass of the one man, how much more did God's grace and the gift that came by the grace of the one man, Jesus Christ, overflow to the many! Again, the gift of God is not like the result of the one man's sin: The judgment followed one sin and brought condemnation, but the gift followed many trespasses and brought justification. For if, by the trespass of the one man, death reigned through that one man, how much more will those who receive God's abundant provision of grace and of the gift of righteousness reign in life through the one man, Jesus Christ.

Consequently, just as the result of one trespass was condemnation for all men, so also the result of one act of righteousness was justification that brings life for all men. For just as through the disobedience of the one man the many were made sinners, so also through the obedience of the one man the many will be made righteous.

The law was added so that the trespass might increase. But where sin increased, grace increased all the more, so that, just as sin reigned in death, so also grace might reign through righteousness to bring eternal life through Jesus Christ our Lord.

Our choice is actually quite simple: Do we want to receive the gift of forgiveness through what Jesus Christ did on the cross, or do we want to pay for our sin ourselves and be eternally separated from God?

We receive forgiveness of our sins through faith in what Jesus Christ did on the cross and by submitting our lives to Him as our Lord and Savior. He becomes our Savior when we put our faith in Him, because of the work of the cross; He becomes our Lord when we choose to place Him in charge of our lives. They go together, and when we put our life under His leadership, we establish Christ as our foundation, both now and for all eternity.

Your Foundation

We've all seen the aftermath of earthquakes and the damage that was caused by them. Some buildings crumble while others are left standing. The reason some stand is because their foundation was strong enough to bear the stress of the earthquake. All the buildings were put to the test, but only those with the strongest foundations stood.

In a similar way, all men face stress in their lives. Some men are able to go through it, still standing when it is all done, while others crumble and fall. Standing up to stress means staying faithful to your spouse, being disciplined to go to work each day, working hard, and maintaining a moral and spiritual focus. Crumbling means you take the easy way out, giving up on your marriage, getting drunk or high, or even immersing yourself in pornography to hide from the stress. At some point in our lives, we will all face trials and storms, but my question is, will what you are building stand, or will it be washed away by the pressures of life? Jesus lays it out simply for us:

"Therefore everyone who hears these words of mine and puts them into practice is like a wise man who built his house on the rock. The rain came down, the streams rose, and the winds blew and beat against that house; yet it did not fall, because it had its foundation on the rock. But everyone who hears these words of mine and does not put them into practice is like a foolish man who built his house on sand. The rain came down, the streams rose, and the winds blew and beat against that house, and it fell with a great crash." (Matthew 7:24–27)

What is your foundation today? You may have picked up this book because you want to be a better husband or a better father; maybe you want to build a legacy that sees your children and grandchildren blessed; or maybe you want to impact society and change the culture in which you live. Those are all noble reasons to have picked up this book, but the game plan Jack and I are sharing begins with Christ as the foundation of your life. Have you ever begun a personal relationship with Jesus? I'm not talking about going to church or "being spiritual." Rather, I am talking about Jesus being your Lord and Savior.

If you want to begin a personal relationship with Jesus Christ today, you only need to pray a short prayer from your heart.

Jesus, I want to be on your team and for you to be my foundation. I want you to lead me and be in charge of my life. I want to begin a new life today following you. I know I have sinned and been separated from you. Thank you for dying on the cross to pay for my sins. I put my faith in you and the work of the cross to pay for all of my sins, and I ask for your forgiveness. Please strengthen me each day to follow you. I pray in Jesus' name, amen.

Once you have a strong foundation in place by accepting Jesus Christ as your Savior and Lord, it's time to start building. Are you ready to begin?

PRAYER:
IT ALL STARTS HERE

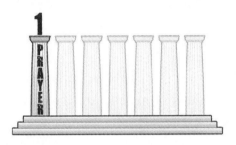

To be a Christian without prayer is no more possible
than to be alive without breathing.

—MARTIN LUTHER

You want something but don't get it. You kill and covet,
but you cannot have what you want. You quarrel and
fight. You do not have, because you do not ask God.

—JAMES 4:2

Caution: This is the most important chapter in the book. It may
scare you away.

If you struggle to make prayer a significant part of your life,
know you aren't alone. Most men doubt the power of prayer, or
they are bored by the thought of sitting still and talking to someone they can't see. A lot of you might be tempted to stop reading

now because you aren't interested in praying longer or harder. However, don't let this challenge keep you from reading on. This chapter has the possibility to change your life. You're a man, so if something is important to you, then you will do it. If you're serious about building a legacy, then you must be serious about being a man of prayer.

Legacy-Minded Men Choose Prayer

A legacy-minded man must be a man of prayer. Only through prayer can we discover, experience, and achieve God's purpose for our lives. It is only through prayer that we can leave a solid legacy for the people we care about. And it is only through prayer that we can create a spiritual legacy that will bless our families for generations to come. Prayer is one of the most important things we can do. But from years of experience, I can tell you that prayer is not something men do naturally. It's often not their go-to play when the chips are down; it isn't their go-to when life is good either.

I (Jack) have talked to a lot of people who are mad at God. They have a problem or situation they want God to change, and He hasn't yet done what they wanted Him to do. So they rant and rave about the situation, and they blame God for not helping them. The funny thing is that when I ask them if they have prayed about their problem, often these same people look at me with a dumbfounded expression and tell me no.

Most people want things and will go to extreme measures in order to get them. They quarrel, fight, and even kill, as the Bible says, but they never take the time to pray and ask God for help. We have two choices to make whenever we face circumstances in our lives: we can either face our problems with our own strength and ability, or we can turn to God in prayer so we can face our problems with His strength and ability. The choice is really up to us.

Choosing to look for God's strength in prayer is just the first step. After we choose to be a man of prayer, we then need to learn some important lessons. We have to learn to invest effort in something that doesn't come naturally to us, and we have to learn humility in the process.

In general, men are doers, not talkers, and the simplest definition of prayer is talking to God. God has wired us to get things done, and we resist sitting around running our mouths when we could be doing something much more "productive." However, in order to pray we must learn how to spend time talking to God.

Grace and Power through Humility

Men like to be in charge—we want to fix things; we want to win. But prayer takes us out of the driver's seat and puts us in the passenger seat. It requires us to admit that we need God's help, which is humbling. Most people I know resist humility. But in God's eyes, humility is not optional. We must learn humility or we will be taught humility the hard way.

James writes, "But he gives us more grace. That is why Scripture says: 'God opposes the proud, but gives grace to the humble'" (James 4:6). A great definition of *grace* is God's empowering strength for us to do what He called us to do and to be what He has called us to be. The Bible is clear when it comes to receiving grace. If we want that kind of strength in our lives, then we've got to get over ourselves and be humble.

So what is humility anyway? The Bible gives a straight answer: "Do not think of yourself more highly than you ought, but rather think of yourself with sober judgment, in accordance with the faith God has distributed to each of you" (Romans 12:3). Humble

27

people don't try to impress others or themselves by showing off. They see themselves clearly, as people whose best quality is their faith in God, and they shut up about the rest. Isn't that counter-cultural to everything we are taught?

Humble? Missed that class.

Make-myself-look-good-at-all-costs? I got an A+.

To be honest with you, this is where I (Joe) stumbled most. I thought way too highly of myself. I now know this, but it was a painful lesson to learn because when God wants you to see something and you continually refuse to see it, then He will get your attention, and He will get it fast.

The reality is that it takes more strength to be humble than it does to brag. Any guy can shoot his mouth off and act like he's the man; anyone can be arrogant and try to do things solo. Bars across our nation are filled with guys who act like they are ten feet tall and bulletproof while their marriages and lives stink. It's harder to be humble and ask for God's help. So be tough, suck it up, and be a man. Be humble before God.

Kill It and Grill It

Men who want to pray must learn to resist their natural inclination to act first and talk later. The desire to act is built into men by God Himself, and it's valuable. But that same wiring, apart from God's help, can keep us from being the men of prayer God wants us to be. As men, we are at our best when we are being led by God, and not just by our urges and inclinations.

Those instincts run deep. Have you ever heard of the hunter-gatherer societies? Men were the hunters, which meant that the survival of a man's family depended to a large extent on his willingness and ability to get things done. Our culture has mostly eliminated the need of hunting for survival, but we would argue that accomplishing important tasks and achieving career goals are our modern-day hunting.

Men want to see the prey, kill it, drag it home, and then grill it. We don't want to sit around at a fancy restaurant talking about how the steak was prepared. We want to devour it. By nature, we are doers. Unfortunately, however, prayer seems like a lot of sitting around. We want in on the action. Thankfully, God gives us the opportunity, because prayer is the key to kingdom action.

Real prayer is not passive. It is the way we aggressively take hold of what God has for us. It's the way we kill it and grill it in the Spirit. When we pray, we are in the ring, in the fight, bare-knuckled and bleeding. Praying is action, and it is where true victory is really won.

Be All God Created You to Be

The Bible is clear that God has a purpose for each and every one of us. He made us to do "good works" that He prepared in advance (Ephesians 2:10). Amazing, right? But choosing not to pray limits that purpose. Apart from God's power we are limited. In our own strength, we can never do all that God created us to do. We must learn to become men of prayer if we will ever become men of legacy.

You can learn this the easy way or you can learn it the hard way. Unfortunately, I (Joe) chose the hard way. If you asked me what motivated me to become a man of prayer, the answer would be simple—pain. Yup, you got it. In my failure—pain. In my inadequacy to change myself, people, and situations—pain. When I looked into the mirror and didn't like what I saw—pain. When people who loved me criticized me (and I knew they were right)—pain.

Many times I came to the end of myself and lost the game I was playing. I was forced to realize that without God's serious involvement in certain situations, I was going to lose and keep on losing. In prayer, I discovered that God could and would change me, and then use me to change the situation. My future victory could only be guaranteed if it was won in prayer.

Learning to Pray

If we truly want to be legacy-minded men, we must learn to be men of prayer. It's a challenge, but it's not impossible. It's also not a cookie-cutter skill. The way one relates to God in prayer looks different for each person. Jack and I are no exception. Looking at our prayer patterns might help you create your own prayer style. The point is to do whatever works for you.

Honestly, I (Joe) don't often have "prayer times" in the traditional sense of praying at set time periods, and I'm okay with that. For me, prayer is more of an ongoing conversation that I have with God throughout the day. Here is what works for me: "Rejoice always, pray without ceasing, in everything give thanks; for this is the will of God in Christ Jesus for you" (1 Thessalonians 5:16–18 NKJV).

My prayer life tends to follow this Scripture. I try to live in a state of praise for all that God has already done for me, and He's done a lot. Throughout the day, I communicate to God that I am thankful for the new day, my job, my family, and all of His blessings. I think that my willingness to praise God is a good test of my spiritual health. If I can't heap praise on the one who gave me life, then I need to conduct a strong examination of who I really am and what I really believe.

Thankfulness has helped me to keep my sanity through all of

life's ups and downs. It reminds me of all that God has done, and how good He truly has been to me. It makes me smile and places hope in my heart. Thankfulness also keeps me from getting discouraged by all of the problems in my life and in the world.

In addition to praising and thanking God, I also ask Him for things throughout the day. There are always a million thoughts running through my mind, and so I turn those thoughts into prayers. When a thought about a man I've been working with pops into my head, I turn this problem into a prayer. When I start to stress out about a bill I can't pay or a resource I don't have, I turn that concern into prayer. I don't waste time worrying about what I don't have or haven't been able to do. Instead, I invite God into the situation and ask Him to take care of it.

When I meet people who are overwhelmed with their situations, I don't tell them I will pray for them later—I do it right then and there. Too many of us say we will pray for someone, but with all the distractions around us, or from a simple failure to care, we don't follow through. So I try to pray while the request is fresh in my mind, because this honors God and the person who made the request. It has become my habit to constantly turn these problems and needs into prayers when I'm asked so I don't forget to pray for them later.

Apart from praise and requests, I also like to talk with God. He is my Father and He is always there for me. He already knows everything that's going on in my life, and everything about me, so I don't have to hide anything from Him. I come to Him, just as I am, and talk to Him.

Another prayer habit I've developed is to keep a list of prayer requests. As a business owner, husband, and father, I have a lot of concerns, and a lot of requests I can bring before Him throughout my day. At Legacy Minded Men, we spend our time and effort reaching out to men who have "man" issues. As I interact with these men, I learn about their needs and challenges, and my prayer list grows. Over the years, I've learned to take care of my business and let God take care of His. So as I pray throughout the day, I continually trust that God hears and is working things out behind the scenes.

This lifestyle of prayer has resulted in answered prayers, which has encouraged me to keep praying. Prayer invites God into situations that seem hopeless. There are certain things only God can truly change, and that's why I pray.

Prayer Works

It was the summer of 2007, and my (Joe's) son Jordan, who was then twelve years old, was on his first mission trip. He went to Oswego, New York, to help rebuild a home. On one of the last days of the trip, he was working on the ground floor. His job was to pass four-by-eight foot pieces of 5/8-inch plywood to the second floor, and then the workers on the second level would in turn pass the sheet to the third floor.

At the end of the day, Jordan and his team leader shoved a final sheet up to the guys on the second floor. But when the crew on the second floor pushed it to the third level, no one was there to catch it. The third floor crew had mistakenly thought they were finished and weren't in place. Since there was nobody to grab it, the sheet of plywood plummeted back down to the first floor. Those who saw it yelled, "Run!" The team leader escaped, but my son tripped and the piece of plywood fell directly on his leg. The damage was significant. His leg was crushed, and his foot was actually dangling by the ligaments.

My wife, Bethanne, and I got a call about the accident while

Jordan was on his way to the hospital. When we asked what the damage was, they said it was most likely just a broken or fractured leg. And they told us not to worry. Bethanne got in our van and said, "I'm driving!" Then she drove like a bat out of hell to get to the hospital. On the way, we got a call from the doctor, who told us that Jordan needed surgery right away to remove pressure on his leg. The operation was done while we were still en route. They could not wait for us to get there because they feared that the bone was going to break through the skin if it continued to swell.

Fractured leg? Yeah, I don't think so. By the time we arrived at the Oswego hospital, Jordan was out of the operating room, lying groggily in a hospital bed. Unfortunately, because of the swelling, they couldn't put anything on his leg in terms of a cast. He was in a tremendous amount of pain, so we stayed in the hospital with him that night. The next day, we drove him to our local hospital where he could see a pediatric specialist. Because Jordan's leg didn't have any protection, he felt every bump we hit on the ride there.

The specialist gave us bad news: Jordan might never walk again. To make matters even worse, he told us the piece of plywood had gone through the middle of Jordan's growth plate, which probably meant his leg would stop growing. It also meant that in order to keep both legs the same length, they would have to break Jordan's other leg, limiting its growth as well.

We refused to believe this report and turned to the Creator in fervent prayer (James 5:16). We prayed hard, and we told the doctor that, regardless of the prognosis, Jordan was going to be made whole again. This boy had been significantly covered by prayer since before he was born, and we chose to continue to put his life, and his body, into the hands of the God we had learned to trust.

Later that year, when the cast finally came off, Jordan walked again. The doctors were amazed! What's even more amazing is that Jordan played ball that next spring. He was able to pitch, hit, and run the bases. Not only that, but he has grown almost a foot since the doctors told us his growth plates were too damaged to allow him to get any taller.

As I write this, Jordan is just over six feet, the tallest member of our family. How could this have happened? Jordan's recovery defied the doctors—they could not understand how it happened. The answer is simple: prayer is powerful and it works!

Prayer as Relationship

For the first ten years or so of my Christian walk, I (Jack) wasn't consistently passionate about prayer. I prayed, and God answered many of my prayers, but, in reality, I was failing the humility test. I was thoroughly engrossed in pride. Instead of evaluating myself based on the faith God gave me, as God tells us to do in Romans 12:3, I was comparing myself to other people. I concluded that I prayed as much or more than many of the people I knew, so I felt pretty good about myself. I was absolutely "thinking more highly of myself" than I should have.

Comparing ourselves to others is a dangerous game we often play. Because I was "doing some things better" than the people I knew, I was satisfied. I didn't really think I needed to focus on growing in my prayer life. But then I met some powerful men and women of prayer. When I compared myself to them, I realized I was like an all-star on a junior high basketball team—not a starter in the NBA.

As we described earlier, men like to get things done, and I'm no exception. At times, I have seen prayer as the turboboost button my life. When I want to get big things done, then I need a big boost so I pray a big prayer. So I would be passionate about a situation and pray until it was "fixed," but after that I was done. At times, I wanted God's power more than I wanted Him.

The pastor of my church challenged me to ask myself an important question: Am I a man who prays or a man of prayer? When I first heard the question, my inadequate prayer life was screaming at me. Yes, I prayed, but I could not call myself a "man of prayer." Since hearing that question, however, I've been growing in the area of prayer. Certain things only happen with time, and certain things require lots of time if you want a deep and rich experience. I have learned to make prayer a greater priority instead of making my works for Jesus the priority.

Set the Clock for Prayer

My (Jack's) prayer life hinges on two things. Like Joe, I love to pray throughout the day as different things are thrown at me, but I also build times for focused prayer into my daily schedule. If I am going to spend significant times in prayer, I have to schedule them. What do I mean by that? First, I try to pray for thirty minutes each morning. I get up, go to my kitchen, put thirty minutes on the timer, and pray until it beeps. Some days I get distracted and skip my prayer tiime, but for the most part this is my morning routine. I also schedule days of prayer and fasting throughout the year. This may seem rigid, but it's what I have to do; otherwise I will work and barely pray.

Like any new skill, at first it was tough to pray for half an hour, but over time it has gotten much easier. Many days now, the thirty minutes fly by, and sometimes the thirty minutes don't seem long enough. There are many times I just keep going until I "feel" like I am done.

To grow, I had to challenge myself. I had to stop accepting the status quo of my spiritual life. If I could watch a two- or three-hour game on TV and not spend a half hour with my Lord and Savior, then my priorities were not lined up. I'm not saying there is anything wrong with watching a ball game—invite me over; let's eat some hot wings—but mature faith and spiritual legacy don't happen by watching a football player make a tackle or score a touchdown. It only comes by being a man of prayer.

Seasons of Prayer and Fasting

As a new Christian, I (Jack) was so excited about all that God was doing in my life that I wanted more. Every time I did something my pastor or other leaders in the church told me to do, it was like my spiritual life was turboboosted to the next level. So in 1998, when my pastor declared that the church was going on a ten-day fast, I was in. It was a partial fast, which meant I could eat one meal a day but skip the other two. The idea was that in addition to your regular prayer time, you would use the time you normally spent on those missed meals to pray instead.

I went for it—no breakfast and no lunch. I read my Bible and prayed instead. The solution to problems I was facing in life became much clearer, and I felt God more during those days. Over the years, I have continued to fast periodically, sometimes just skipping two meals, while at other times foregoing everything but water. I can honestly say that every time I have fasted, I have experienced growth, greater clarity, and increased closeness and leading of the Lord.

Fasting has been especially helpful when I needed spiritual renewal or help in breaking down Satan's strongholds like lust, anger, or unforgiveness. Fasting weakens and pushes the flesh down while strengthening your spirit. This allows you to overcome the flesh, be healed, and become more like Jesus.

Legacy-Minded Men Are Men of Prayer

Legacy-minded men don't stay stuck in discouragement; they turn their problems into prayers and watch God turn their situations around. Yes, prayer is work. One reason men avoid it is because they perceive prayer as passive, but when men deliberately engage in times of prayer, they find out that it's hard work, and many of them give up.

Becoming a man of prayer will not happen by accident. It takes training. Just as an athlete works on a physical challenge, prayer is a spiritual challenge that takes much effort. Even though it is hard, it is well worth it. The recipe for spiritual victory always includes prayer.

As men, we face a constant flow of demands, problems, and crisis situations. So we have a choice to make: we can tackle these problems in our own strength, or we can pray for God's help. Just like the plates of pasta a runner eats before a marathon, prayer is our fuel to keep going.

By establishing the pillar of prayer, you can bring God into every situation you pray about. On your own, you are limited. Prayer invites God's constant presence and infinite power to bear on your problems. It is also a key part of building the other pillars of your legacy.

Just a Thought

Is there someone in your life you really want to learn from? If you could meet with that person every day, for as long as you would like, would you do it? Of course you would. In the same way, you can spend whatever time you wish with the *Creator* of the universe. The question is, why don't you?

Pillar Builders

- Be ready to pray all the time.

- Have a list of prayer items.

- Constantly thank God for what He is doing in your life.

- Set a deliberate time for prayer each day.

- Establish times of prayer that include fasting throughout the year.

Additional Study Verses

- 1 Chronicles 4:10

- 2 Chronicles 7:14

- Psalm 141:1

- Jeremiah 29:11–13; 33:3

- Daniel 9:3

- Matthew 5:44; 6:5–9

- Mark 11:24

- Luke 11:1

- John 14:14; 15:7; 16:24

- Romans 8:26

- Philippians 4:6

- Colossians 4:2–3

- 1 Thessalonians 5:16–18

- James 4:2–3, 6; 5:16

- 1 John 5:14

- Revelation 5:8

PERSONA:
WHO YOU ARE IS WHO YOU ARE

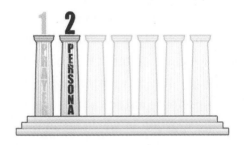

Be yourself: everyone else is already taken.
—OSCAR WILDE

The position a person occupies in the world depends
on the quantity and the quality of the service he renders
plus the mental attitude which he relates to others.
—ANDREW CARNEGIE

Hello World, This Is Who I Am

Your persona, or your personality, is how you portray yourself to others. It is a combination of your gifts and talents, preferences, thoughts, and attitudes. In fact, your persona determines your tendency to act in a certain way in any given situation. You can think of it as your default way of interacting with the world. Are you loud? Quiet? Helpful? Irritable? Do you act like a grumpy old man or a rich young ruler? Are you more of a leader or more of a follower? This all comes from your persona.

Some people use their persona to hide who they really are. There is little consistency between their inner and outer lives; their personality is simply a mask. Casinos in Las Vegas have mastered the trick. One with an Eiffel Tower pretends to be Paris; another with a Statue of Liberty masquerades as New York; and a casino built like a massive pyramid imitates Egypt. They're all facades. Visitors, no matter how much they want to believe otherwise, are still playing slots in the middle of the Nevada desert.

However, a man of integrity with a healthy persona doesn't wear a mask. His persona portrays who he really is, all of the time, no matter the situation in which he finds himself. Ideally, our personalities honor God and bless others. But sometimes they don't. Our personalities have been shaped by our surroundings and experience, our upbringing, our trials and struggles, our victories and our failures. So we must put this warning here: results may vary.

There is good news and bad news about persona. The bad news is that by the time we are adults, some parts of our personalities are pretty much set. But with the right input, a lot of the aspects of our personas can be shaped and changed, which is the good news.

Will the Right Persona Please Stand Up?

Many men are confused about who they are supposed to be. The ideal male persona has been the subject of a lot of debate. On one hand, men are told to be strong providers who never waver. Then, in the next breath, they are told to be soft and sensitive.

They are bombarded with contradictory demands that no one person could ever hope to live up to.

In an ideal world, every boy and young man would be surrounded with caring adult role models who could point the way to the right persona. Sadly, though, we are living in a far from ideal world, and many men flounder in a jumbled mess of mixed messages about what manhood truly is. Lacking role models and teachers, even men who accurately determine their target persona still struggle to create it. They are often expected to know things and act in ways they haven't been taught.

This is where God makes all the difference. He purposely created and gifted you to be *you*. Your strength is in that, not in some manufactured personality that someone else wants you to adopt. Jumping through hoops to make people happy may work temporarily, but it is no way to live the majority of your life.

We are shaped, for good or for bad, by our upbringing, and we are at our best when we have a strong character and a great attitude. But there is a sweet spot in how God wired us. As legacy-minded men, we need to live out the persona God intended us to have.

Persona Improvement Plan

Attitude and character are two critical aspects of our persona. Luckily for us, both of these respond well to training. *Attitude* consists of the feeling, disposition, or the orientation of mind we have toward a person or thing. The classic example is of two people who both look at a glass of water. One person smiles and declares the glass half full, while the other frowns and declares it half empty. The tendency to see the glass as full or empty is in our attitude.

One of the best ways to begin working on your attitude is to first notice it. A lot of times, people just feel how they feel. That is to say, they don't really ask themselves if a different mind-set is possible or even desirable. As believers in Jesus, we have a lot of reasons to have a good attitude: God has promised to be with us always; He has given us His Spirit to live inside of us; He has given us power over our sinful tendencies; and He loves us unconditionally. Armed with those truths, men can face their present situation and their fears for the future with an assurance of hope. They can, as the saying goes, "Keep calm and carry on." That's the kind of attitude that characterizes a legacy-minded man.

The other indispensable aspect of persona is *character*. According to the dictionary, character has three aspects to it: it's the sum of all the parts that add up to who we are, it's our moral or ethical behavior, and finally it is our reputation.

J. Oswald Sanders, in his classic book *Spiritual Leadership*, underlines the importance of character. He wrote, "Every Christian is under obligation to be the best he can be for God."[2] As legacy-minded men, we need to take character development seriously. If we want to have the best possible character, then we have to get serious about how we act around other people. Are you likeable, friendly, and positive? Or are you difficult to talk with, hard to get to know, or whiny? If you fall into the second group, then it's time to change. No matter how entrenched these behaviors are, you can do better.

Being serious about character also requires a zero-tolerance policy when it comes to bad morals or ethics. Not many of us will attend military school, but the cadet honor code at West Point can guide us ethically. It says, "Don't lie, cheat, steal, or tolerate those who do."

Finally, think about your reputation. Do people trust you?

Should they trust you? If your mistakes in the past have left you with a bad reputation, then it's time to start building a new one. Go to the people you have hurt and ask for their forgiveness. Tell them you are sorry. But don't just stop there: you must rebuild trust by showing people that you are trustworthy. Start small: be on time for work; take out the trash when you are supposed to; pay your bills on time.

While it's certainly possible, and many times desirable, to work on our personas is not always easy. We need the help of our friends.

The Power of Your Inner Circle

Many men are distant from their spouses and have few, if any, close friends. They lack the right people in their lives to help them achieve spiritual, business, or financial success. These men suffer from the Lone Wolf syndrome. They are Lone Rangers without Tonto, Tarzan without Jane, George Steinbrenner without the Yankees. People survive like this, but they don't flourish. God did not create us to be lonely, unsupported, or disconnected from others. Our inner circle has a huge impact on the quality of our life—emotions, fulfillment, spiritual walk, and financial status.

Friends can make or break our persona. The negative impact of friends is spelled out in 1 Corinthians 15:33, where Paul reminds us, "Bad company corrupts good character." But the reverse is also true: good company promotes good character just as powerfully. Friends will push us to be better or help us be worse. Who we choose to spend time with matters greatly. John Maxwell, in his book *The 21 Irrefutable Laws of Leadership*, says, "Every leader's potential is determined by the people closest to him." [3] We not only agree with Maxwell, but we would expand that law to include every legacy-minded man.

I (Joe) understand the Lone Ranger way of thinking because I grew up as a loner. I was a loner as a businessman, and I didn't have any close, confiding relationships until much later in life. Until Legacy Minded Men became a reality, I did not realize the negative impact of my Lone Wolf status. For the first time I truly realized I needed to be part of a team. I was ready to surround myself with solid men. In many ways, Legacy Minded Men exists because I needed it more than anyone.

Because of my past, it was a bumpy process. Until Legacy Minded Men began, most of the people who said they "cared" about me usually only did so because they wanted something from me. As a result of those experiences and relationships, I struggled to differentiate between people who were playing me and people who truly cared. Over time, however, the Lord has made it easier for me. The test I use is this: the people who truly care about me keep coming back and asking how I am doing, no matter my personal circumstances.

One such person is my good friend Jim Henry. When I was recruiting men to be part of what would become Legacy Minded Men, a friend of mine suggested I contact Jim. We met shortly after that, and I poured the vision out to him. The whole time, he listened but did not react at all. Because I'm an emotional Italian, I took his silence as a sign that he was disinterested. But when I finished, he finally spoke. To my surprise, he said two simple words: "I'm in." I was ecstatic! Since then Jim has become a second father to me, a man for whom I will do anything. My inner circle was being built.

Your Dad: The Key to Your Inner Circle

Your relationship with your dad sets the "norm" for you. God's purpose for fathers is to establish norms, boundaries, and behaviors that are both godly and wise. According to Proverbs 22:6—"Train up a child in the way he should go: and when he is old, he will not depart from it" (KJV)—fathers are supposed to train their children in godly ways, showing their kids how to navigate through life.

Many men have benefited from the influence of great fathers, but others have been left floundering because they didn't have a dad who taught them how to live as a man. Sadly, the number of men who grew up without the influence and teaching of an involved father is growing. According to the US Department of Justice, "Fatherlessness is a growing problem in America, one that undergirds many of the challenges that families are facing. When dads aren't around, young people are more likely to drop out of school, use drugs, be involved in the criminal justice system, and become young parents themselves."[4]

Obviously, more men than ever are left scrambling to survive without the valuable training a good dad gives. These men don't have game plans, or the game plans they do have are faulty. When life's storms hit, these fatherless men don't have a plan, and the most important member of their inner circle—dear old dad— isn't there to lean on.

Persona in Action: A Case Study

Mike Tyson once said, "Everybody has a plan 'till they get punched in the mouth."[5] He was an incredibly gifted fighter with a great work ethic. But that wasn't enough to succeed in life. When he was in a tough situation, his persona fell short. A closer look at his life story shows how the key ingredients for a great persona were not in place for Tyson.

In an autobiographical piece he wrote for *New York* magazine,

Tyson describes his years growing up. According to Tyson, his dad wasn't around and his mother was drunk "all the time." After getting beaten up at school, Tyson quit going—he was just seven years old. Soon afterward, he got involved with a gang and began robbing homes. Then at the urging of other kids, he took up fighting, earning both money and respect. He was arrested often. And at twelve years old, Tyson was sent away to a juvenile detention center.

As a child and young teen, Tyson's inner circle was rotten to the core, but it was all he had. "Some people might read some of the things I'm talking about and judge me as an adult, call me a criminal," Tyson wrote. "But I did these things over 35 years ago. I was a little kid looking for love and acceptance, and the streets were where I found it. It was the only education I had, and these guys were my teachers."[6]

At the juvenile detention center, Tyson met Cus D'Amato, a boxing trainer who would change his life. D'Amato promised to make Tyson "the youngest heavyweight champion of all time."[7] He recalls that comment from D'Amato as the first time he ever heard anyone say something nice about him.

Tyson's inner circle now included D'Amato. The older man definitely helped Tyson win, but the influence was geared toward boxing. "Cus wanted the meanest fighter that God ever created," Tyson wrote. "He trained me to be totally ferocious, in the ring and out."[8]

When D'Amato passed away, Tyson was left floundering. Divorces and bankruptcy, a rape conviction, and prison followed. Like so many other men, Tyson didn't have a father to teach him basic life skills. He failed often, publicly, and damagingly. While he was alive, Cus had protected Tyson, but he hadn't left him the kind of legacy Tyson could rely on. His lack of an inner circle in his private life led to the downfall of his career.

Perhaps the most graphic illustration of the character weakness Tyson struggled with occurred during the 1997 World Boxing Association Championship fight with Evander Holyfield. Tyson was in a tight spot, and he responded like the "meanest … totally ferocious" fighter that D'Amato had trained him to be: he bit off the top of Holyfield's ear. His boxing license was temporarily suspended and he was disqualified from the match.

Trading a Bad Persona for a Worse One

We can all criticize Tyson and other celebrities for their lack of or their bad persona, but the reality is that it took me (Joe) a couple of tries before I got it right. You may be in the same boat.

Growing up, I was an awkward kid with a lot of pimples. As I've said, I was often a loner. I had friends but no close relationships. I liked girls but wasn't exactly the most popular guy with the ladies. I had pretty low self-esteem. And all of this led to a conclusion: I would give myself a personality makeover before I went off to college. No one at my school had known me before, so I saw the start of my college days as an opportunity for a personality do-over. So I decided to reinvent myself.

What new persona did I choose? The big-mouth guy who showed off at every opportunity. I was convinced that some girls would like it, and I thought that this particular persona would earn me respect from other guys. And you know what? It worked.

A couple of positives came out of my improvement experiment. I learned that it was possible to change my persona and other people's perceptions of me. I also learned that I was more of a leader than I knew. But the new me had a dark side too. I became really good at being a shallow jerk. The new persona was simply a facade to mask my insecurity—it didn't solve the problem; it just kept it out of sight. The result of all my effort to change my persona amounted to a temporary fix for an immature kid. Instead of having character, I became a character.

My Big Mouth Helped Me Not Get a Job

It took me awhile to figure out that the "new and improved" Joe wasn't a winning persona. When I was around twenty-three, I was a hotshot staff accountant (is that possible?) at the Witco Chemical Corporation. It was my first job. My aura at the time was that my poop didn't stink—other people's might, but not mine. So I decided to venture out and look for a new job. A headhunter set up an interview for me in a nearby town. Though I don't remember the name of the company, I sure remember the meeting.

My interviewer was a young guy who immediately made me feel confident and comfortable. About halfway through the interview, I planted my feet firmly on his desk. We talked about women, partying, and all of my considerable conquests. When I left, he gave me a slap on the back and told me he looked forward to seeing me soon. I left feeling absolutely positive I had gotten the job. When I arrived home, however, there was already a message on my machine. The call was from my headhunter.

Her first message was this, "Joe, I just heard from the company and, unfortunately, you did not get the job." When I heard those words, my heart sank. The rejection didn't make sense to me. I thought I had connected with the interviewer on a "spiritual" level. But the next words that came out of her mouth changed the way I looked at myself from that point on. She said, "Oh, by the way, he has a message for you: 'Grow up!'"

During the interview, the interviewer was testing me. He wanted to see how far I would go. He opened the door, and I just ran my mouth. What was impressive to a twenty-three-year-old whose life was a mess was unimpressive in the real world. Based on my record, I was qualified for the job. I had the skills and a passion that seemed like a slam dunk for success. But what I lacked was a good persona. I was undisciplined and my priorities were out of whack. My carefully cultivated college persona let me down.

What I needed was another persona overhaul. But this time, I needed the help of an inner circle of people who would encourage me to develop a godly attitude and character. Until that time came, my persona was a liability.

When Life Hits

We said earlier that persona is our default way of interacting with the world around us. My (Joe's) default persona was on display when I felt comfortable in a job interview. But oftentimes our default persona is most clearly revealed in times of crisis. For Tyson it was the fight with Holyfield, while for others it's a loss, a financial struggle, or a temptation.

Who are you in those moments? Do you default to anger or confusion, drinking or drugs, pornography or illicit sex? The truth is that without an established character, a good attitude, and a strong inner circle, the survival instinct will kick in, and you may find yourself doing stupid things to cope with the pain. But if you have the right inner circle and a strong personality, you will default to good character and a positive attitude, dust yourself off, and modify your game plan.

Tragedy and crisis hit all men. Your persona will either rise up to keep you going or crumble under the pressure. The fact is that you *will* get hit, but the question is, what is your plan when you do? When you squeeze an orange, tomato juice does not come out—only orange juice. It's much the same with all of us— when we are squeezed, the real us comes out.

Just a Thought

You can't turn back the clock or erase the past. In this chapter I (Joe) shared some stories from my life that make me wish I could go back and have a do-over. But real life isn't like that. There are not many times where we can have a do-over. Below are the three areas that make up your persona. We may not get do-overs in all areas, but God does give us new days to do things differently. If you could fast-forward one year from today, what would these three areas look like, and what would you change about them?

Pillar Builders

- Attitude:
  1. What needs to change?
  2. What are you specifically willing to do to change in your attitude?

- Character:
  1. What is the biggest area of character you need to change?
  2. List at least three actions you can take to build a stronger character:
     a.
     b.
     c.

- Inner circle:
  1. Are you connected with and surrounded by the people you need to be a legacy-minded man?
  2. What type of people do you need in your life to be everything God created you to be and to do

what God created you to do? Here are some areas where we all need coaching (quite possibly different coaches based on the area):

a. Spiritual
b. Successful singleness
c. Husband and father
d. Financial and career

3. How can you find and include these people in your life?

4. If you want to find out who you really are, then take a piece of paper and list your strengths on one side and your weaknesses on the other. Be completely honest with yourself. Then share your list with someone you love and trust. Ask them to review your list and provide you with honest feedback. Hold on tight, and if you hear something you don't like, decide beforehand you won't go nuts. Maybe you can learn something about yourself.

Additional Study Verses

- Proverbs 5:22; 12:5; 14:12
- John 3:30; 8:44; 14:6
- 1 Corinthians 1:24–31; 15:33; 16:13–14
- Philippians 1:27; 2:3; 4:8
- 1 Peter 5:8-9

PURITY:
THE PATHWAY TO GOD'S PRESENCE AND POWER

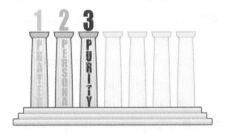

Most men usually have one of two weaknesses—
money or honey.

—Anonymous

The concept of purity isn't a big hit at most bars or ball games, and it doesn't come up a lot in boardrooms either. But where God is concerned, purity means the difference between being connected or disconnected from Him. That connection matters because we are blessed and transformed in His presence. Apart from the transformation that takes place in His presence, we are on our own. This is why the psalmist declared:

Who may ascend the hill of the Lord?
Who may stand in his holy place?

He who has clean hands and a pure heart,
>who does not lift up his soul to an idol
>or swear by what is false.
He will receive blessing from the LORD
>and vindication from God his Savior. (Psalm 24:3–5)

A legacy-minded man takes personal purity seriously. In fact, he has to. It's the main area where Satan attacks most men. Purity paves the way to connecting with God, being in His presence, and intimately knowing Him. Sin and a lack of purity do the opposite—keeping us from God's presence, love, and power.

To put it simply, if you purposely live an impure life, you will be on your own. You will have chosen your sin instead of God. Your legacy, instead of resembling the glory of God, will resemble you—in all your impurity and brokenness.

In the past, when people used the phrases, "You are a chip off the old block," or "You are just like your father," it was a compliment. Now, because our culture has become so impure and broken, when a mother yells, "You are just like your father," it typically follows some type of personal failure, and it's often a slap in the face.

Hand or Heart Sanitizer, Anyone?

Clean hands and a pure heart are the recipe to connect with God on a regular basis. Clean hands represent the things we touch, the things we choose to do with our lives. Are our hands committed to our wives only, or are they the tools that search out Internet pornography and cause us to dream of other women?

A pure heart represents what we love. Is our heart filled with affection for God and His people, or is it filled with greed for money? Do we trust God to provide for our needs, or are we cooking the books at tax time? Is our next car or next house more important than God? Do we cringe when our pastor asks us to support the church or a missionary because it would mean sacrificing tickets to the next ball game? If our answer is yes to any of these questions, then those things—the tax refund, the house, the car, the game—have become idols. They are occupying our hearts and dirtying our hands.

In Exodus, the Bible tells us how God's people decided as a group to make an idol. They went to Aaron and demanded that he make a golden calf so they could bow down before it and worship. In our day and age, we don't usually take a vote and petition Congress for something concrete to worship, but we do let idols creep into our lives, making us impure. Over time, these misplaced loves and wrong actions pry us away from God.

Psalm 24:5 tells us that God's concern for our purity is broader than simply stopping us from sin. He wants to bless us with joy. So often we think of God as an angry boss who is looking for an opportunity to fire us. Instead, we need to see God as the ultimate coach. When good coaches tell a player what not to eat, set a curfew, or require wind sprints, it's because they want him or her to win. And they want to celebrate in the victory.

God is like a good coach. He not only wants to save us from sin, but He wants to be a continual blessing in our lives. A clean heart and pure hands are the sure recipe to receive and fully enjoy that blessing.

Money or Honey: What's Your Poison?

It has often been said that men have one of two weaknesses: either money or honey. Let's be clear here: God often provides us with both. If you are called to be married, then God wants you to have a great wife and a solid relationship with her. And God clearly tells believers that they are to provide financially for their families (1 Timothy 5). Proverbs is full of advice that can make a business grow or an employee succeed. But in our spiritual battle, the enemy of our soul will always try to take what God has given us and twist it for his purposes. He wants to use good things for our destruction.

I (Joe) am a businessman. I work hard to make money, and so should you. I am also married and enjoy the benefits of having a physical relationship with my beautiful wife. But as a believer, I have to guard myself against greed and lust; I have and still can struggle with both. The world teaches us to wrongly pursue sex and money, and our flesh sometimes desires them too. Ironically, if we indulge our flesh and obey the world, we are poised to lose the good blessings—loving wives and good jobs—that God has so graciously provided.

Dad's Sex Talk

Personal purity is another place where our relationship with our father—or our lack of relationship—has a huge impact. In a perfect world, we would all grow up in a healthy family with two parents who are fully committed for life to each other and who demonstrate and teach us all the things we need to know. The reality is often much different, however. Lacking that parental guidance, the world, the flesh, and the devil start a tag team wrestling match that often lands us outside of God's boundaries and leaves us with dirty hands and a stained heart.

Unfortunately, like a lot of parents, my (Joe's) dad didn't give me a lot of advice about sex and relationships. But when I went off to college, he decided to throw in his two cents. As I was getting ready to leave home, he delivered his entire version of sex education in two words. He simply said, "Be careful."

That was my dad's entire life's wisdom on teaching his son about sex—all two words of it. Telling an eighteen-year-old boy to be careful about sex, then setting him loose at college with no rules, no morals, and hundreds of women is like telling a hungry shark not to eat, then throwing bloody fish parts in front of him. It shames me to say that I did not even follow those two simple words, although I wish I did.

One guy I know has taken teaching his sons about purity a lot more seriously. He purchased a curriculum from a Christian bookstore that begins with teaching about body parts and goes from there, covering puberty and God's design for sex in marriage. He handles the formal "sex talks" differently with each kid.

One of his boys is a little more reserved, so he just gives him the material to read, then follows up with an opportunity to ask questions. There usually aren't any, and that particular kid appears to be totally embarrassed by the whole process. My friend isn't put off by that. He wants his son to have good information, and he wants to be the one to provide it. It's a legacy issue.

The other son is more open, so my friend announces the next sex talk with a little more fanfare. They read through the books out loud together, with the kid adding helpful comments like, "No way!" and, "Are you kidding me?" With this kid, it's all my friend can do to hold it together and not laugh at his son's reaction. Again, it's a legacy issue.

In this family, these formal sessions help to keep sexuality an open topic. A lot of times, if an adult brings up an issue, kids will perceive that the subject is safe to talk about.

The method used to pass down biblical sexual values will vary from family to family, but the important thing is to make sure it happens. Very few kids are going to sit down with you at dinner and ask about your sex life. The responsibility for telling them what they need to know about God's plan for sex is on you, their father. If you just can't make yourself go there, consider delegating it to your wife, or enlist another trusted adult.

If you don't teach them, life will, and it won't be a good education. Make biblical teaching on sex available to your sons, and make your legacy a good one. I wish I had done this better with my own children.

Yankee Chapel: From a Liar to a Legacy-Minded Man

Purity doesn't just have to do with sex; it also has to do with the motives of our hearts. I (Joe) learned this in a very costly way. When I was a young Christian, just out of the gate, I was asked by Dave Swanson, the head of Baseball Chapel, an organization that brings church to minor and major league stadiums around the country, to speak to a group of seventy-year-old men.

I had been taught to pray before you speak, asking God for the words. Once a person had prayed, then he or she was to just let it rip. For me, the formula sounded like this: prayer + open mouth = impressive message. So that's what I did. In His kindness, the Lord blessed me, and I sensed Him speaking clearly through me. There was not one "ah" or "um." It was an awesome time, and when it was over, many of the men came up to me and said things like, "Young man, keep talking," and "Boy, did you encourage me." I went home pumped up.

The following day Swanson asked me to speak at the Sunday chapel service at Yankee Stadium prior to the scheduled game between the Yanks and the Baltimore Orioles. I knew that speaking to a bunch of seventy-year-old men was an entirely different ball game than speaking to the New York Yankees. I had been having a lot of interaction with players as I researched my first book, *Safe at Home*, but this was different. This was speaking to these men on a spiritual level.

Dave didn't take no for an answer. The next morning after breakfast, we jumped in the car and headed to Yankee Stadium. Swanson showed me to the room where I would speak, and he let me know that there would be two sessions: one for the Yankees and one for the Orioles.

Following the same plan as my last talk, I went to the men's room and prayed to the Lord. *Take me over just like the other day*, I asked. *Speak through me.* Then the Orioles came in and once again, it was awesome, everything went perfect, and there were no "ahs" or "ums"—it was flawless. The guys slapped me on the back and said, "Well done." Again, I was pumped.

There were fifteen minutes between the Orioles' chapel and the Yankees' chapel, but instead of going back into that men's room and praying, I walked around. I paced around in circles thinking, *Wow, I'm really good at this. This is something I'm really good at. I'm as good as my pastor. Maybe I can be the next Billy Graham!* Before I knew it, the door flew open and seventeen Yankees walked in. I knew some of them, and I was happily thinking, *You guys can get ready to be blessed.*

Dave introduced me. I had the floor. I opened my mouth and nothing came out. I forgot everything I was going to say, and I started a "hummina, hummina, hummina" kind of thing. Lacking anything else to present, I started telling the story of how Dave and I met. At the time, I guess I thought it was an important and spiritually edifying story. It might have been, but I also embellished it *juuusssst* a little bit. I stretched the truth so badly that Dave interrupted me and said, "That's not true." That was a major-league "ouch!" Whenever I speak, I always tell people that if you want to be humbled, then be called a liar publicly while doing chapel for the New York Yankees!

What we say comes out of our hearts, so our words are a great test of the purity of our hearts. Jesus said, "For out of the abundance of the heart the mouth speaks" (Matthew 12:34 NKJV). This means that truthfulness is one of the first and best tests for the purity of our words. When you lie, you are connecting yourself with the father of lies—the devil (John 8:44). When you tell the truth, you are connecting yourself with Jesus, who actually *is* the truth.

Purity or impurity are also a lot like snowballs rolling down a hill. The longer they roll, the bigger they get. When we lie, we open the door for the devil to have power in our lives. Believe me: it just makes the lying snowball more massive. On the other hand, telling the truth shuts out the devil and opens the door for Jesus and His power to come into our situations, creating one holy snowball of truth.

I Was Working on a PhD in Lying

As I (Joe) said earlier, when I was a kid, I told many lies because I wanted to be somebody—somebody I wasn't. When I was small, I was scrawny, so I got beat up. I got taken advantage of. Anybody who has had those experiences knows they play in your head. They make you angry and they cause you a lot of angst in social situations. And so I handled all of this by lying when I was young.

People lie because they want something they don't have or to avoid something that is painful. I wanted to be stronger than I was, and I wanted to avoid the pain of being weak and inferior to those around me, so I lied. One of the reasons people lie is because it works—at least for the moment. Just like a house of cards, lies will stand up for a while and look good, but as soon as that first gust of wind hits, they topple. That was my pattern early on: build a house of lies and hope I wasn't around when it crumbled.

Remember, our legacy is our pattern. If our lifestyle is a mess, then our legacy—what we leave for the people who follow us—will be too. We will wake up one day to see our kids repeating or "improving" on our sins, making them worse than ever. In effect, we teach our kids how to sin. As legacy-minded men, however, we need to see our own purity as a priority so we can help our kids avoid sin by leaving them a legacy of pure living.

Teaching My Son to Lie

Early in my (Joe's) parenting life, I had a chance to see my lying transferred to my son. My wife and I took our small children to Hershey Park in Pennsylvania. Joey was three years old, and Jennifer was about a year old. Our funds were low, so I paid attention to a sign that said kids two and younger didn't have to pay admission.

As we got close to the gate, I picked up my son and whispered in his little ear, "If they ask you how old you are, say you are two." I carried him to add to the illusion. Sure enough, he got in free. It was a great day at the park.

Remember how we said that in stressful situations we resort to our default persona? Standing in line at the park, I was stressed. I was wrestling with the shame that I didn't have a lot of money. As men, we often feel that money is power, and when we lack money we feel powerless. When I felt like I didn't measure up financially, I went to my default persona—a frequent liar. Without even knowing it, I was building that kind of default legacy for Joey.

On the way home, we stopped on the New Jersey Turnpike for a burger. My son, who was incredibly cute and talkative, began chatting with the people in the next booth. The lady sitting there asked how old he was, and I'll never forget his answer: "Well, I'm three years old. But when I go to Hershey Park, I'm two." Man, did I feel like a worm.

> There is a way that seems right to a man, but its end is the way of death. (Proverbs 14:12 NKJV)

You see, telling my son to lie "seemed right" while I was in line. "It's only a little lie," was the popular phrase running through my head, as was the reality that my wallet was light. In the end, the money I saved wasn't worth it. Something in me died when I realized that I had used my son and taught him to lie just to save a few dollars.

But my sin and my mistake taught me something too: my character was impure, and it needed to be disinfected by the gospel. There was a lying side of me that needed to be buried. I had a choice: would my legacy to Joey be the impure example of a habitual liar, or the pure example of a godly man who honored truth? The change had to begin in me.

Thank God that He didn't give up on me that day. Even though I knew I needed to change, it wasn't until Jesus empowered me that I really did change. I've learned that if God does something for someone else, then He surely can do it for me too. You can be confident that if God changed me, then He can also do it for you as well.

Just a Thought

When I (Jack) moved into a new neighborhood, I quickly became friends with my beer-drinking, constantly cussing neighbors. I was a little different—I had quit cussing and drinking when Christ saved me years before. Behind my back, they started joking about me. Then they challenged each other not to curse. Someone broke out a coffee can, and they made a bet. Every time one of them cursed, they had to put a dollar in the can. That lasted for about a weekend until they stopped because they couldn't afford their habit. I would laugh and remind them that without Jesus they'd be stuck with their potty mouths forever. The coffee can had proved it.

You may not struggle with lying or cussing, but there is probably some area of your life that requires some fine-tuning at the least, or maybe even a total overhaul. Here are a couple of questions to ask yourself to get the ball rolling in the right direction.

- What is it that I want to change when it comes to purity in my life?

- What steps should I take to walk this out in my life?

Pillar Builders

One of the ways you can maintain purity is to have certain things in place to protect you from impure thoughts and actions. One way to look at these are as "purity protectors." When we play football, we wear equipment to shield us from injury. In life, we have insurance to guard us and to help us when things get tough or go wrong. A legacy-minded man builds purity protectors into his life, and he teaches his sons to do the same thing. Here are a three "purity protectors" that every man can build into his life.

- Friends:
  1. Who in your life really knows you?
  2. Who can ask you the hard questions?

- Accountability partner: This can be huge in helping you stay on track. This is a must if you have a history of pornography, drug or alcohol abuse, or other ongoing issues. An accountability partner is someone who has your permission to know your personal actions and thoughts and to help you avoid impure actions. Here are ten great questions for your partner to ask you and for you to ask him:

1. How are you doing with God?
2. How are you doing with your mate or the person you're dating?
3. How are you doing with your children?
4. What temptations are you facing and how are you dealing with them?
5. How has your thought life been this week?
6. Are you consistently living for Christ in your workplace or at school?
7. Have you been spending regular time in the Word and in prayer?
8. With whom have you been sharing the gospel?
9. Have you lied in your answers to any of the questions above?
10. How may I pray for you and help you?

- Wife: You should not have to hide things from your wife. For long-term intimacy, she needs to trust you, and you need to trust her too.

Additional Study Verses

- Job 31:1
- Psalm 24:3–5

- Proverbs 4:25–27
- Matthew 5:8; 12:34
- Luke 8:17
- Romans 12:1–2
- 1 Corinthians 6:9–12; 7:9
- 2 Corinthians 10:5
- Ephesians 4:30
- Philippians 4:8
- Colossians 3:5
- 1 Thessalonians 4:3
- 1 Timothy 5:22
- Hebrews 13:4
- 1 Peter 2:11
- 1 John 1:7; 3:3

PURPOSE:
UNLOCK WHAT YOU
WERE CREATED TO DO

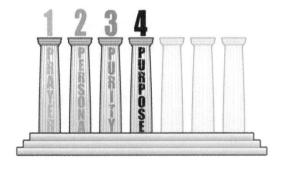

Don't be afraid to give up the good to go for the great.
—JOHN D. ROCKEFELLER

You can be marked by the past or make
your mark in the future. The choice is yours.
—ANONYMOUS

What Is Your Purpose?

A few years back, *The Purpose Driven Life* by Rick Warren broke
record sales as thousands of churches embraced the importance
of teaching about purpose, and tens of millions of people bought
the book. Warren's simple message was received with passion

because the average Joe struggles to know if he is living out his purpose.

It might be difficult, but knowing God's purpose for our lives is worth the struggle. When we know our purpose, we can handle disappointment without growing discouraged. We can hit home runs when life throws us curveballs, we can protect our relationships from unnecessary conflict, and we can do what we know is right even when our decisions seem crazy to other people. All of these benefits come from seeking and following God's purpose.

To be clear, there are two types of purpose: general and specific. Every man's (and woman's, for that matter) general purpose is to:

- Love the Lord your God with all your heart, soul, and mind, and love your neighbor as yourself (Matthew 22:37–39)

- Share the good news (Matthew 28:19–20)

- Remain pure (1 Thessalonians 4:3–8)

But his specific purpose is unique to him. A legacy-minded man seeks out his specific purpose, looking for the reasons God put him here on earth at this time in history. Then, once he finds his specific purpose, a legacy-minded man gets to work fulfilling that purpose.

Guidance from the Book of Jeremiah

There are two Bible verses from the book of Jeremiah that make five things clear about our purpose in life. As you read these, picture God speaking these directly to you:

Before I formed you in the womb I knew you,
    before you were born I set you apart;
I appointed you as a prophet to the nations.
(Jeremiah 1:5)

"For I know the plans I have for you," declares the LORD,
"plans to prosper you and not to harm you, plans to give
you hope and a future." (Jeremiah 29:11)

1. *God made and formed you.* Just as a sculptor shapes a lump of clay into something he can use, so God actually shaped us and formed us so that He could use us to accomplish His purpose on the earth. God's plan in creating us resembles that of an engineer who designs something with a form and structure to meet a specific purpose. That's what God has done for each and every one of us. Our existence is not a random event. God has shaped, molded, and designed us for a purpose. We all go through times when we feel bad about ourselves, but these verses powerfully remind us that no one is an accident or a reject. God made us for a reason.

2. *God knew you before you were formed.* God is all-knowing, which means He knows everything about us and has known everything about us since before the time of creation. This gives us two choices: we can either ask Him to show us our purpose, or we can fumble through life, trying to figure out things for ourselves. Sometimes we are surprised by a weakness in our character, or, on the positive side, we discover a hidden talent and wonder how to use it. These things weren't in God's blind spot. He knew about them all along. And He's ready to use them as part of His purpose for you.

3. *God has set you apart for a purpose.* Our culture, the media, and our educational system try to drag us on to a man-made path, forcing us to just "go along to get along." The world's system tempts us because it's popular. But at the end of the day, it's not the right thing for people who are set apart by God.

One of the reasons so many men have a midlife crisis is because they bought a ticket to the system's path early on, and when they get halfway to their destination, they suffer buyer's remorse. These men have spent their lives working toward the system's goals and dreams, only to end up disappointed. In an effort to regain lost time, true purpose, and meaning, they often throw away the first half of their lives and hurt the people they have met along the way. Jeremiah reminds us that God's purpose for His people is different than the one the world promotes.

4. *God already knows the plans He has for you.* The question of purpose is not an unsolvable mystery, and we don't have to figure it out by ourselves. Some men look for their purpose like kids trying to hit a piñata at a birthday party. Blindfolded and dizzy, they are holding a stick, hoping their next swing will connect with their purpose and not one of their friends. However, God's way is much different. He knows the purpose He has for us, and He wants to let us in on it. Our challenge is to walk with Him and talk with Him, learning His purpose as we go. We need to take off the blindfold (and put down that stick).

5. *God's plans are to prosper you.* People often think they can come up with a better plan for their lives than God! They act like they can out-create the Creator and out-plan the Planner. Others don't know or understand that God created them with a plan and purpose, so they just go with the flow, doing whatever seems right at the time. Still others, lacking a firm grasp on what God wants from their lives, are easily caught up in the schemes of

people. Many of them get used or abused. But these verses teach that God's plan for us is good, giving us hope and a future.

How to Know Your Specific Purpose

God's path is not a dead-end street. For us legacy-minded men, He already has planned a future that brings great hope and success. However, some of you may be wondering, *How do I know my specific purpose?* In addition to searching Scripture, three things you can do to help you understand your purpose and achieve it are:

1. *Define what you are passionate about.* Generally, we are driven internally by a purpose given to us by God. Some questions to ask yourself are: What do I love? What do I dislike? What is that thing that wakes me up at night or the first thing I think about when I get up? Many times, our purpose is connected to what we are most passionate about.

2. *Define what you are good at.* There is a difference between a hobby and a purpose. Many of us love to do certain things, but we may not be the best at them. To live the greatest life means to have the most possible impact. When you take a hard look at your talents and abilities, you will likely discover your life purpose.

3. *Receive trusted feedback from others.* When you surround yourself with the right kind of people, your inner circle, they often give you solid feedback on who you really are. I am not saying to listen to everyone. Still, who do you have in your life that has experience and wisdom? I (Joe) have experienced that when I spend time with the right people, they see my gifts in ways I did not see myself. I would not be where I am today without this encouraging feedback in my life.

It is important that we have a firm grasp on our general and specific purposes as we go through life and face its many storms.

This knowledge can act like an internal GPS to keep us going through the ups and downs we all face.

Responding to Disappointment

It is easy to get caught up in the lure of a dream or a goal. When it doesn't work out, we get discouraged and forget to look for God's specific purpose. I (Joe) experienced this about two years into my career. I was working with a headhunter to find a new job, and I interviewed at the Sealed Air Corporation.

Learning from my previous mistakes, I was both professional and polished this time. I left feeling confident that the job was mine, but when I got home the headhunter called and said, "I'm sorry, Joe. They chose someone with a little more experience, but they really liked you and want you to come back to interview for a different position." Believe it or not, that scenario repeated itself three times. I ended up interviewing four times at the Sealed Air Corporation, and I never got the job. After the fourth interview, I was devastated—I bawled my eyes out.

The next day, a seemingly random phone call that was a wrong number put me in touch with another headhunter. She took advantage of her mistake to drum up business by asking if I was looking for a job. You betcha! Through my new headhunter, I interviewed at another company and met the controller, Arnold Kezbom. Kezbom and I hit it off, and he hired me. I ended up following him to three jobs, each time getting a substantial raise. The whole experience gave me a well-rounded business background that provided the confidence I would need to eventually run my own company.

Before my success working with Kezbom, however, I had tried hard to get a job at Sealed Air, and I suffered a great deal of pain when I was rejected there. But God's specific purpose for me was different. He did not want me to work in the accounting department at Sealed Air. He wanted me to work at smaller companies where I could get experience and learn how to run a business.

I didn't see the silver lining when Sealed Air turned me down over and over again. In fact, most people don't when they are in the midst of a bad situation. But I've learned to keep my eyes open a bit wider, and you should too.

Handling the Unexpected

Things don't always go according to plan. Unfortunately, when situations veer away from the expected, we feel unprepared and uncomfortable. Knowing and understanding our purpose can take the sting out of those moments. When we know our purpose we have a plan, and when we pursue our purpose we get prepared for the plan. The unexpected becomes an opportunity. I (Joe) learned a lot about this when life threw me a big, public curveball.

Sometime after I began the Legacy Minded Men ministry, I was invited to a Hispanic pastors' banquet in Jersey City, New Jersey. I didn't know a lot about the evening, but I wanted to be a part of honoring these men of God for their service. I had been busy and I was tired. I looked forward to the event as a time to relax, have a nice meal, and spend time with some men of God.

You can imagine my surprise when I arrived at the banquet and saw my name listed in the program as the keynote speaker! At first I thought it was a mistake, but after further investigation I realized it wasn't. With no advance notice, I would be called on to deliver the big message of the night. So I did what any man would do in that situation: I called my wife and asked her to pray.

This wasn't some preseason game. I run a ministry for men, and the leaders I would address that night represented thousands of men. I clearly saw how my performance that evening could cause Legacy Minded Men to explode to the next level of influence or be a roadblock that could stop it in its tracks. No pressure! I had no time to prepare a great message, so I had to trust in my persona, experiences, and, most importantly, God.

And He delivered. In the moments before the event began, as I fervently prayed, God gave me the words to say. Despite the language differences and short notice, I was able to deliver a strong message in an uncomfortable situation. It was clear that God had a plan all along—to make connections that could impact Hispanic men in the days ahead. He just didn't tell me all the details beforehand.

I realized something important that night. While I may not have had advance notice about the keynote speech, I wasn't totally unprepared. I had history with God. I had spent years growing in my relationship with Him, and He had spent years preparing me for both expected and unexpected ministry moments. I had been soaking up Scripture for a long time so that in the situation the Holy Spirit could pull it out of me, at just the right time.

It was a powerful night, one I will never forget. I'm thankful for the unexpected opportunity, and I'm glad I was prepared. I had already discovered and pursued my purpose, which was to help transform lives by engaging, encouraging, and equipping men to build a Christ-centered legacy. My question to you is, when life throws you a curveball, will you have what it takes to stand in the box and hit it out of the park?

Protecting Relationships

Our purpose has the power to protect our relationships. This is especially true when the people we care about make mistakes that cost us time, money, or effort. I (Joe) learned a lot about this aspect of purpose a couple of years ago. It was a stressful time for our family. In August of 2011, my home was flooded, and our family was forced to move into a hotel for ninety-nine days.

Our vehicles still worked, and that was important because my son was learning to drive. Flooding, relocation, and driving lessons with a teenage boy—you could say I was wound a little tight.

One day I took Jordan to an unfamiliar parking lot to practice his driving. He began well. But when he attempted to park, he didn't notice the little brick divider at the front of the space. When he finally did notice it, instead of hitting the brake, he accidently hit the gas. And the car jumped the curb. When the car landed on the island, I screamed, "No," and Jordan, more nervous now than ever before, stepped on the gas again, leaving the car teetering on the island with its wheels hanging off either side. None of the tires were touching the ground.

I asked Jordan to get out of the car, and I took over at the wheel. I gunned the engine, and the car flew off the island, but it was banged up. The back bumper had been pulled out, the exhaust system was about two feet longer than it should have been, and there were a lot of little things damaged. In my mind, I was going insane. The car was brand-new. But I also knew that how I handled the situation could hurt my son's confidence.

As I drove around a bit to see how bad the damage was, I prayed: *Lord, this has got to be a teaching experience. I don't want him to be afraid to drive because of my reaction. Lord, help me to respond well.* When I calmed down I drove back to Jordan. I got out of the car, walked to the passenger side, and told him to get in and continue to practice driving.

"Dad, I'm really sorry," he said.

"It's not your fault," I replied. "Don't worry about it."

Because I understood that my purpose as a dad at that particular moment was to instill confidence, I was able to use the moment to teach him, not scar him. The situation could have driven a wedge between Jordan and me, but instead it solidified my purpose as a father. My purpose is to teach him and to be his biggest fan.

Sadly, as a parent, there have been too many times when I did not respond well. On this particular day, however, knowing my purpose helped me do the right thing and get through a rough day with a significant relationship intact.

Bizlink

Sometimes knowing your purpose causes you to act in a manner that other people don't understand. Your purpose may lead you down a hard and difficult road, and other people will think you are crazy for staying on the path. The opinions of other people aren't what matters most in your life—you were made by God for a purpose, and it's your responsibility to fulfill that purpose, no matter how painful it is.

I (Joe) got a taste of how hard fulfilling a purpose can be in 1998. I was the co-owner of a weekly newspaper with a mailed circulation of 70,000 pieces and $2 million in annual sales. Despite our success, my partner and I knew that the business climate was changing, and so we decided to sell. The Internet and corresponding tech stocks were booming, and we took advantage of that opportunity, selling the paper to a tech company for a stock deal worth about $1 million.

I thought it was a really nice deal, and it provided me the

opportunity to start my dream business—a multimedia company called Bizlink. Bizlink was cutting edge and exciting. Investors thought so too, and we effortlessly raised $1.3 million for the start-up. New York Yankee legend Don Mattingly became our spokesman and one of my partners. It was a thrilling time!

But in April of 2000 things started to go wrong. The market crumbled, and there were internal problems at Bizlink. The company went bankrupt just six months later. There were two groups who were hurt in the bankruptcy: employees and investors. I worked hard to find jobs for the employees. At one point I was offered a new job as a COO in a company. I thanked the person who offered me the spot, but asked him to use the salary he would have paid me to hire two of my former employees. He agreed and hired both men. All my former employees found work, but I was still unemployed.

I had lost all my savings in the deals, and because the tech company that purchased my paper for a stock deal went belly-up, I had nothing to show for the once valuable asset. And I wasn't the only one to lose out. As part of the corporate bankruptcy, roughly $200,000 in company debt would be written off. But I knew the people who had loaned Bizlink the money, and I didn't want them to lose their investment. I just could not let that happen.

I talked with my wife, and we decided to personally take on the company's $200,000 debt. Our balance sheet looked like this: no job, a big mortgage, three kids, and $200,000 in extra debt. Help me, Jesus! Some people urged us to declare personal bankruptcy, but we didn't think that was part of God's purpose for us, so we didn't.

Enter Life and Leisure

The decision not to go bankrupt and to take on the debt put us under a great strain. It was an extremely hard time. I (Joe) did a lot of jobs to earn income, but there was no clear solution or path forward. It was only by God's supreme grace that we made it through. To be honest, I have no idea how—the numbers just didn't add up, but the bills got paid. It was a God thing.

In August of 2003, we decided to move from New Jersey to Georgia, where housing costs and taxes were much lower. Our reasoning was simple. We thought our home in New Jersey would sell for around $500,000. With only half of that money, we could get a great house in Georgia and use the difference to pay off the debt to our Bizlink investors. Turns out that wasn't God's purpose for us either.

Shortly after we made the decision to move to Georgia, I was contacted by the owner of another paper, *Life and Leisure*. The man, whose name is George, told me he wanted me to help him start a new paper. I told him that I felt God was leading me to Georgia and he said, "No, no, you don't understand, God wasn't saying Georgia; He was saying 'George.' 'I'm leading you to George.'"

George won me over, and we agreed to begin the new newspaper. Knowing the amount of work involved, I was reluctant but did not want to stand in the way of God's plan. That willingness to follow God's purpose paid off. As we moved forward with *Life and Leisure*, God helped us overcome obstacle after obstacle. At one point, we were required to prepay for our postage and printing, but we didn't have any money. A newly hired employee offered the money from a home equity loan she had just gotten. As everything lined up, I realized that God had His hand on this venture. Now, more than fourteen years later, we are still publishing *Life and Leisure*. God has blessed that paper and my family through it.

There have been other times when I have had to choose to stick with God's purpose, despite other people's opinions of me.

At one point, I was offered $350,000 for *Life and Leisure*. Yes, the money would have gotten us out of debt, but the man who wanted to buy the paper told me that he would take all of the Christian information out of it. So I opted not to sell.

I still remember the look on a good friend's face when I told him that I was going to turn the deal down. It was clear that he thought I was crazy. Looking back on it now, I think God blessed that decision. A few years later, I sold 49 percent of the company for roughly the same amount I had turned down. I was able to pay off the majority of the debt that we had incurred from Bizlink and still have the company. It also provided the door to open Legacy Minded Men.

The lesson is this: fulfill your purpose, *regardless* of what other people think.

Just a Thought

The graveyard is the richest place on earth, because it is here that you will find all the hopes and dreams that were never fulfilled, the books that were never written, the songs that were never sung, the inventions that were never shared, the cures that were never discovered, all because someone was too afraid to take that first step, keep with the problem, or determined to carry out their dream. —Les Brown[9]

Have you ever sat down and really thought about your purpose? If God created you for a purpose, what is it? What are you doing to get there? Are you going to live out your dreams and purpose, or are you going to take it with you to the grave?

Pillar Builders

Write out a list of goals, such as:

- Before I die, I will …

- In ten years, I will …

- In five years, I will …

- In one year, I will …

- Within the next thirty days, ask someone to coach you in at least one area of your life to help you achieve your life's purpose.

One of the greatest things a man can do to achieve his purpose is to sit down with others who have already done what he is dreaming about doing. Ask those successful people what they think about your plans. Does your gift set fit your dream? In what areas will you need help? Do you have the right short- and long-term goals? Maybe they can coach you or recommend someone else who can. But remember that there is no consultant more in tune with your purpose than the God who created that purpose in you.

Additional Study Verses

- Exodus 31:3–6; 35:10, 35

- Esther 4:14

- Proverbs 19:21; 20:5

- Jeremiah 1:3; 29:11

- Luke 12:48
- John 18:37
- Acts 6:2
- Romans 1:1; 8:28; 12:6
- 1 Corinthians 7:24; 9:16
- Ephesians 2:10; 4:1
- Philippians 1:6, 12; 3:12
- 2 Timothy 1:9
- Hebrews 12:1
- James 4:17
- 1 Peter 4:10

PRIORITIES:
YOU NEED A PLAN OF ATTACK

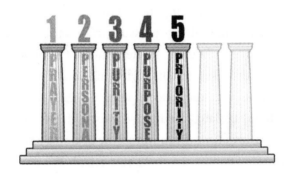

If you fail to plan, you plan to fail.
—HARVEY MacKAY

The Tyranny of the Urgent

Life is busy. Incredibly busy. The days of working 9 to 5 and being able to retire at fifty-five with a nice pension may be gone forever. Endless things pull at us and beg for our attention. It's easy to have nonstop days and booked evenings. One would expect to have something to show for that much activity, right? But when we look back at our busy days, we often struggle to identify any worthwhile accomplishments.

Culturally, we have more luxuries and less time, more social connections but fewer real relationships. People have more access to us, which leaves less and less free time to engage in the things we enjoy. Economic forces drive many people to work harder than ever just to survive. Many of us aren't trying to keep up with the Joneses, we are simply trying to keep food on the table. At the other end of the financial spectrum, some people have more money and possessions than they could ever use but they feel like their lives have no meaning.

Either way, we are challenged with navigating our schedules and making sure we are living the life that God created us to live. Unfortunately, there is always pressure from our culture to compromise or strive to live out its definition of success. At some point, we can get sucked into lifestyles that don't bring God glory.

We've all had the experience of working really hard for something only to realize later that it wasn't worth the effort. Instead, it was a huge waste of time. Even worse, the goal was often achieved at the expense of something more important. We got sucked in, and we sacrificed our priorities for some type of busyness.

Charles E. Hummel, whose career included work as the faculty director of the Christian ministry Intervarsity Christian Fellowship, and served as the president of Barrington College, wrote a short booklet titled "The Tyranny of the Urgent." In it he said, "We live in a constant tension between the urgent and the important."[10] Urgent things scream for our attention, Hummel wrote, but truly important things—time for Bible study, prayer, reading good books, and serving the poor—don't.

The booklet was published in 1967. In it Hummel describes how telephones installed on the walls of homes robbed people of a quiet place that was free from interruptions, where they could focus on and accomplish the important tasks. Imagine what Hummel would say about today's world where most people have access to the Internet, voicemail, text messages, Facebook, and

Twitter, all in a pocket-sized device. Our technology makes the urgent more tyrannical than ever. Learning to recognize goals and stay focused on them is an important part of becoming a legacy-minded man.

The Tension of Priorities

You've got a mortgage to pay and you've got kids to feed. You're trying to make it all work. But why doesn't it? We have to manage the tension of the reality of these needs without neglecting what our heart is telling us is the most important.

The truth is that most men already know what's important. Married guys would say it's important to spend time with their wives, and fathers would say that their children are important. But many of these same men have not figured out how to establish a regular date night with their wives or spend more than a few minutes a day in conversation with their children. Eventually, many wake up in a house with a discouraged spouse who feels neglected and a distant teenager. Neither of these is God's will or produces a great legacy.

Then how do we close the gap between what we "feel and believe" is most important to us and the reality of how we spend our time? The simple answer is this: make a plan and stick to the plan. The plan takes a big idea like "love my wife," and breaks it down into concrete actions to accomplish. Thinking out concrete steps to accomplish our priorities is an area where most of us fail. We don't plan to focus on what really matters, with the result that our lives are consumed by too many nonessential things.

As adult men, we need to remember what it was like when we played football, basketball, or another sport. We had a plan. We had a playbook and memorized the plays; we had practices scheduled and went to them; we scheduled gym time and worked out. But when it comes to our priorities, we often don't win because we have no plan. It's not that we are not trying, it's only that our energies are spent somewhere else. When it comes to what matters most, we run out of time or have no more fuel in the tank.

Once we have a plan in place, we have to stick to it. When God wanted Moses and the people of Israel to remember the Ten Commandments, He carved them into stone. That's how we need to approach our plans for the important things in our life. That date with your wife or talk with your kid can't be changed on a whim; keep it written in stone. Legacy-minded men learn to build a plan to succeed at what matters most. Setting nonnegotiable priorities allows us to navigate a world of never-ending demands.

Two events stand out in my mind when I (Joe) think about living by a set of priorities. In the first, my clearly defined priorities and a serious commitment to stick to them, no matter the cost, kept me from hurting my little girl in a way that could have left lasting damage. In that situation, I knew what to do because I knew my priorities and I had a plan. Let's take a look at a time when I got it right.

A Father's Love

During the 1998 World Series, first baseman Tino Martinez swung his bat and changed the entire complexion of the contest between the New York Yankees and the San Diego Padres. Clearly, this was one of the most exciting games the Series has ever produced, and to have it occur in New York made it even bigger.

I (Joe) have been a serious Yankee fan since I was about ten.

Quite frankly, the Yankees were the first thing I ever really locked onto. During a difficult childhood in which I had no self-esteem or self-confidence, baseball became my release and the Yankees the object of my affection. Years have passed, but my affection for the Bronx Bombers burns strong. I still receive a tremendous amount of pleasure watching the team play and following their progress. My passion for the Yanks has been strengthened by the opportunities I have had to get to know many of the players through Baseball Chapel. I also got close to the baseball scene through my first book, *Safe at Home.*

Since I have been a fan, the Yankees have been involved in twelve World Series, including the magical season of 1998. I made a determination that year that the team was good enough to get to the Fall Classic, and I was going to make it a point to be there to cheer them on. To guarantee a spot, I purchased a partial season ticket plan, which gave me two tickets for every Friday night game at the stadium. It also assured me of two seats for the first game of every playoff series, including the World Series. I attended the first two playoff series and had an incredible time.

However, just about the time it became apparent that the Yanks were headed to the World Series, my wife, Bethanne, mentioned to me that our church was having a father-daughter dinner.

"Great," I replied. "When is it?"

"Saturday, October seventeenth."

I immediately cringed, thinking that the date could also be the first game of the Series. The tickets did not have a date on them, so I called the Yankees, and they confirmed my fear: the first game was on October 17. I then asked the ticket sales representative if I could trade the first game for the second game of the series.

Their reply was simple: "No exchanges! No returns!"

I slumped. My dream of attending a World Series was now in serious jeopardy. What could I do? I called several ticket brokers and asked if they would be interested in trading the October 17 tickets for the following day, a Sunday. They were happy to buy my tickets, but they wanted me to pay two times as much to get a new set for Sunday. The price was too high: not an option. The bottom line became clear: if I wanted to go to the Series, I had to go on October 17.

I talked to the Lord about it, knowing already the right thing to do. My daughter Jenny, who was six at the time, then asked me in that incredible way of hers whether or not we were going to the dinner. At the time she asked, I was reading the sports page. On the front of the paper was a big story on the Yankees with a picture of some of the players. After Jenny asked, I told her something special was happening that night, and I held up the paper and pointed to the picture. Her bright smile faded. She felt I had chosen the game over her.

I couldn't stand the look of hurt on her face. Still pointing to the picture, I smiled and said, "It is a very special night because it is going to be our night!" Her smile returned even bigger than before. I don't know if she knew what I was giving up, but I am sure she knew exactly where she stood in my eyes. It is not something she will ever forget, nor will I.

I will never forget it because five minutes after we got to the dinner, Jenny asked me if we could leave. I calmly got down on one knee, and looking into her eyes I told her that we would be staying for the length of the dinner. And that is exactly what we did.

We arrived home just in time to see Tino hit that grand slam, and it was okay that I wasn't there. After all, I got my money back for the tickets and, yes, even made a little extra. But more importantly, my daughter knew that no game, meeting, or anything will ever be more important than her.

Choosing between Good and Legacy

We need to apply the test of priorities to ministry opportunities as well.

From 1995 to 2008, my wife, Bethanne, and I (Joe) ran a charitable program called Adopt a Child. We worked with the local Division of Youth and Family Services (DYFS) to help abused and neglected kids. Many of these kids had been removed from their homes or were being closely watched by counselors. We wanted to bless them, so we contacted DYFS to see if we could provide some gifts at Christmastime. The social workers agreed and provided us with names and Christmas wish lists.

We promoted Adopt a Child through the newspaper that we co-owned. Many people responded and gave faithfully for many years. We collected gifts at our house so that they could be distributed in a confidential manner. One particular year, we had over 3,000 gifts in our home at one time. The program was a success. Over the course of twelve years, we had over 20,000 children "adopted" and secured approximately 50,000 gifts for those kids.

For a couple of years, we included a copy of the gospel of John with each present, but sometime during 2007 and 2008, Bethanne and I began asking ourselves, *Is this really a benefit, giving a child a gift during Christmas?* Even with the gospel distribution, we weren't seeing fruit. Eventually, we concluded that there was no lasting, eternal value in the program.

Even though people praised us for what we were doing, and we were on the front page of the daily newspaper twice, we knew that it was not the most impactful thing we could be doing with our time and resources. Ultimately, we had to prioritize where we were spending our time, and we decided to pull the plug on Adopt a Child, choosing instead to invest in something with more spiritual impact. That decision led to the formation of Legacy Minded Men.

Sometimes the good can be the enemy of the great. In order to say yes to one thing, we must say no to something else. At times like these, having established priorities is essential to help us think and plan clearly.

A Jar of Rocks and My Overly Hectic Life

A man who was teaching on priorities had a large jar and several large rocks. He placed five or six large rocks in the jar until no more could fit. Then he asked his audience, "Is the jar full?" and almost everyone shouted yes. He smiled and then pulled out a bag of smaller rocks and dumped them in until no more could fit. He said, "Raise your hand if you think it's full now." About half the hands went up. He smiled again, pulled out a bag of sand, and poured it into the jar until it couldn't hold anymore. Then he asked, "Is it full now?" Everyone was more skeptical at this point, and so only a few hands went up. People were beginning to catch on.

Lastly, he pulled out a jug of water and poured water into the jar until it overflowed. He said, "Is it full now?" and everyone shouted yes. He then paused and asked the question, "What was the point of this example?" The answers began to fly: "You can always add a little more," "You should never be satisfied with the amount of things you are doing," and "If you try harder, you can always do more."

The crowd was pleased with itself until the speaker smiled

one more time. "You are all wrong—very wrong," he said. "The moral of this example is this. If you don't put the big rocks in first, you will never fit them in. You see, we often lose in the areas that matter most because our time and energy are spent on the little things that consume our time and energy and keep us from winning when it matters most."

Many people cringed as they realized this was a picture of their overscheduled, underprioritized lives. Their lives were packed with the small rocks, the sand, and the water—their jars were full, but they were not doing the things that mattered most. Interestingly, you can skip your priorities and still seem "successful" to the outside world. But every time I have done so, I have felt like a failure on the inside.

I've gotten it wrong many times, but when I gave up the World Series I was able to take care of two important priorities: I built up my little girl and my wife because I put the big rocks in the jar first. Yes, the Yankee game was important, but it paled in comparison to the smile on my daughter's face. I still enjoyed the home run and the win by the television, but more importantly I won as a father and a husband—which is priceless.

Similarly, when my wife and I gave up Adopt a Child, we were able to put the "big rocks" of sharing the gospel and helping men grow in their faith into the jar. If we had kept distributing gifts, we wouldn't have been able to accomplish what God had placed on our hearts as most important. These were both tough emotional decisions, but I wouldn't go back and change either one.

Just a Thought

What matters the most in your life? What really matters? I would encourage you to sit down and make a list of your priorities. Are you scheduling real and sufficient time for what matters most? Are changes needed? If so, work toward putting those changes into practice. If something matters to you, schedule time to get it done.

God made you to win, and having a written game plan will help you win. I (Jack) have benefitted greatly by first writing down my priorities and then scheduling my day in hour-long chunks of time that are committed to the priorities I listed. It brings focus to what is most important on the job and in life. Legacy-minded men have clear priorities and a game plan to execute them.

Pillar Builders

- List your top five priorities.

- Schedule time working on those priorities. List daily or weekly time that is committed to your priorities.

- In our busy schedules, we often have to say no to something in order to say yes to something else. What are some things you need to say no to so you have the time, energy, and resources to say yes to your priorities?

Additional Study Verses

- Joshua 1:6–9
- 1 Chronicles 28:19–20
- Psalm 1:1–3

- Proverbs 15:22; 24:27; 27:23–27; 29:18
- Luke 14:28
- Philippians 1:21
- 1 Thessalonians 2:2

PERSEVERANCE:
TOUGH TIMES INTRODUCE YOU TO YOURSELF

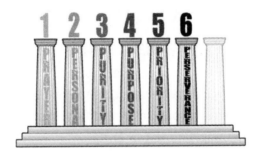

New level, new devil.
—PASTOR JOHN ORLANDO

Pain can be a great teacher.
—JOE PELLEGRINO

Rome wasn't built in a day, and a legacy that outlives you won't be built in a day either. A legacy that blesses your grandchildren and great-grandchildren will take a tremendous investment of your time, energy, and resources. As you seek to build a lasting legacy, you will face trials and temptations. That is to say that you will be tempted to not persevere.

The Bible has a lot to say about how we should handle trials *when*—not *if*—they come. Trials come in many forms: crises, conflicts, or problems. At other times, simply the frustration and the time it takes to get things done can be a trial too. Whatever form your trials come in, if you don't know how to keep going, you can kiss any chance of building a lasting legacy good-bye. Let's look a little deeper at what the Bible says about how we should handle trials and how to persevere through them.

Trials: Our Friend—Really?

James writes about the need for joy in the midst of trials:

> Consider it pure joy, my brothers, whenever you face trials of many kinds, because you know that the testing of your faith develops perseverance. Perseverance must finish its work so that you may be mature and complete, not lacking anything. (James 1:2–4)

We are to count trials and hard times as joy? This Scripture means that we are to welcome trials as friends. Does that mean we should be glad that bad things happen? Well, yes and no. James is not telling us to be a masochist whose idea of a happy life is getting a beat down. To understand any verse of Scripture, we have to keep reading for things to make sense. In verse 4 we see the result of counting our hard times as joy: it is because we become "mature and complete, not lacking anything." Now that's what we're talking about.

Trials help us develop perseverance, which plays an essential role in each of us becoming mature men. Without trials, we won't develop perseverance, and we won't become mature men. Lasting legacies are built only by maturity, not by men who give up every time they face a challenge.

For professional fighters, every loss is a challenge. Yet there is usually one loss in particular that is a turning point in a fighter's career. That loss devastates them because they realize they may have great skills, but they don't have the character or stamina to achieve their dreams. If they don't make significant changes, they will never be anything more than an undercard fighter—they may never get a title shot. Some of these fighters need to switch coaches or camps; others have to get a new diet or new training partners. The bottom line is that fighters who want to win make a decision to make a permanent change.

Are you ready to make the decision to change? If you want to hand down a different legacy to your children than the one you received from your own father, then you need to make the same type of commitment. You need to learn how to turn your trials and losing moments into game changers.

In general, people want the prize at the end of the race, but they don't want to run the race. Others run the race, but they are not willing to put in the training that will qualify and prepare them to win. A legacy-minded man is focused on the end game, the win. He is willing to persevere through whatever life hands him because the prize is worth whatever it takes to get there. A yearlong frustration and trial taught me (Joe) a lasting lesson about perseverance.

The Fourth Time

As previously mentioned, I love baseball. There isn't a better sight than a freshly cut ball field on a warm spring afternoon, and no sound hits the eardrum like the pop of a glove or the crack of a bat. I can trace my love for the game all the way back to when I was ten years old, and my father took me to my first Yankees game. I haven't looked back since.

Ever since, my life has been filled with collecting baseball cards, memorizing statistics, playing games until college, and now watching games. Some might call it an obsession, but to me it is a simple passion. There is something magnificent about this sport we call America's pastime.

You might gather from this that I am a rather passionate person. I'm the kind of guy who falls deeply in love with the things I appreciate. Besides my family, there is only one thing I am more passionate about than baseball, and that is my Lord and Savior Jesus Christ. It took some time for me to understand my need for salvation and to take on this passion toward my faith, but once I did it became my ever-burning fuel.

When I became a Christian, I tried to marry my passion for baseball and my newfound passion for Jesus by writing a book about Christian baseball players. As outlandish as that idea may have sounded to those who didn't share my passions, it made perfect sense to me. So before I began my research for the book, I had a *Field of Dreams* mentality: "If you build it, they will come." I assumed that Christian players would bang down my door to be interviewed for my book. No such luck.

Fortunately for me, one of my business associates was a former New York Yankees baseball player. He was able to wrangle me the "Holy Grail" of major league baseball: *The Major League Baseball Media Guide*. The book contained highly "confidential" information about the teams and players, and it was all mine. I was in my glory.

As I devoured this book, I came across a listing for something called Baseball Chapel. Instantly intrigued, I looked into the listing to find that it was the perfect marriage between my passions for faith and baseball. Baseball Chapel was an organization that commissioned chaplains to conduct short chapels for major- and minor-league baseball teams, and to disciple players who sought discipleship. My knees weakened when I read this.

As I read further, I nearly collapsed. The headquarters for this fount of Christian-baseball goodness was only fifteen minutes from my house. Fumbling for the telephone, I quickly dialed the number that was listed and put in a call to the executive director, Dave Swanson (the same Dave Swanson I mentioned earlier).

The voice that answered the phone said, "Dave Swanson here."

I spilled out my own introduction, and then said, "Mr. Swanson, I love the Lord and I love baseball. I am looking to write a book on Christian baseball players, and I was hoping that you could put me in touch with some of them."

I was greeted with silence on the other end of the line. Finally, he said, "Why don't you go ahead and call me in three months to discuss this further."

Despite the eternity that three months would be, I agreed to his request and waited three months before I called him again. When the calendar finally advanced to the date circled in red with the words *Call Dave Swanson* written on it, I dialed him again. Much to my surprise, he said, "Call me in another three months." Once again, I agreed and marked the date on my calendar.

After three more months elapsed, I called him. To my utter dismay, he told me again to call him in three months. I was confused and more than a little annoyed at this delay, but no length of time would stop me from getting the information I desperately sought. If this was the man who had what I needed, I was going to play by his rules.

Three months later, a full year after my first phone call to Swanson, I looked at the calendar, which indicated it was time to call and receive yet another three-month sentence. Or was it?

"Yes, Mr. Swanson. This is Joe Pellegrino. You asked me to call you back in three months regarding helping me with my book."

His response? "Meet me at the Kin-lon Diner in twenty minutes."

I'm not sure if I actually hung up the phone. Darting up the stairs and into the bedroom, I quickly changed from my dirty gym clothes into a pressed shirt and a tie. Within minutes of the invitation, I was on my way to the diner. When I arrived twenty minutes later, I found a tall, imposing bald man waiting for me at the entrance.

"Mr. Swanson?" I asked. He nodded. I stuck out my hand out, but instead of a handshake, I received a piece of paper. He then turned toward the dining room to find a place for us to sit. As I stared at him in amazement, I glanced down at the piece of paper in my hand. On it were the names of major league baseball players he considered to be strong Christian men. I couldn't believe it. Before he could find a seat, I touched his shoulder.

"Mr. Swanson," I said. "Forgive me, but why now? Why after a year?"

He directed me to a booth. "Take a seat, Joe."

As we sat, I was perked up and ready to listen.

Swanson smiled. "My family used to own the Thomas English Muffin Company. At one time, I was in charge of purchasing. Whenever a salesman called, I never bought from him the first time. If he came back a second time, I still did not buy from him. Nor did I do so if he came back a third time." Mr. Swanson's eyes were glued on mine. "But if the salesman persisted enough to return a fourth time, then he had a customer for life. You just did that."

What a lesson in perseverance I learned that day. So many times we give up or grow discouraged when someone says "not now" over and over again. In many cases, we grow discouraged by even one no. But a legacy-minded man learns to persevere and never give up.

Run Like We Mean Business

In his first letter to the Corinthians, Paul writes, "Do you not know that in a race all the runners run, but only one gets the prize? Run in such a way as to get the prize" (1 Corinthians 9:24). If we are to get the prize, then we have to run like we mean business. Giving up at small obstacles will get us nowhere, but if we persevere, keep our eyes on the goal, and keep running, we can experience that elusive place where success and purpose become one.

Unfortunately, however, many times we give up just when we should persevere a little bit longer. Paul encourages us, "Let us not become weary in doing good, for at the proper time we will reap a harvest if we do not give up" (Galatians 6:9). While some of God's promises are unconditional, many of them give a clear condition that we have to meet. This verse has a condition attached to it. It's like a contract. If one or both of the parties do not meet their side of the contract, then the agreement is nullified. God never breaks His side of the deal, so we're the deal breakers.

Our side of the deal in this verse is to "not give up." We will reap a harvest at the proper time, but God tells us not to give up in order to reap that harvest. Many people are mad at God when something that they hoped for doesn't happen. But they are the ones who didn't follow through with their side of the bargain. They broke the deal and are mad at God. Really?

Hardship is a part of life. We can wish it were otherwise, but the reality is that we all will face trials in this life. This is why Paul writes in 2 Timothy 2:3–4, "Endure hardship with us like a good soldier of Christ Jesus. No one serving as a soldier gets involved in civilian affairs—he wants to please his commanding officer." To leave a legacy, we must endure hardship.

Paul uses the metaphor of the Christian as a soldier who is single-minded in his purpose and does not allow himself to get "entangled" with civilian matters. He is wholly focused on his mission and the battle at hand. Legacy-minded men need that same single-minded focus so that they are able to persevere during hardship.

Other places in the Bible, such as Ephesians 6, make it clear that, as Christians, we are in a spiritual war. One of the reasons the devil comes after men so strongly is because if he can wipe out or ruin a man, then he is able to wipe out or ruin an entire legacy, possibly for generations to come. The many problems and challenges fatherless boys face show what happens when men don't leave a good legacy.

Being a legacy-minded man is not a game. It's not cute. It's not just dressing up and going to church to please your wife. We have an enemy who "prowls around like a roaring lion looking to devour us" (1 Peter 5:8). We need to be on our guard. We need to endure hardship like a good soldier and never forget whom we serve. The race of life is not won by the fastest or the one who looks the best, but by the one who perseveres and builds each and every day.

Just a Thought

On a scale of 1 to 10—1 being an absolute quitter and 10 being "I'll die before I quit!"—who are you? Who are you when life throws everything at you, including the kitchen sink? What are your biggest regrets? Which ones could you go back and fix or do differently? Regret is an ugly thing, but today is a new day for you to do a new thing. This time, however, commit to sticking it out.

Pillar Builders

- What is your most important long-term goal that you will commit to never quitting on?

- What is an area where you feel like quitting but you know you shouldn't?

- In what area of your life do you want purity but compromise when stressed out?

- Who do you have in your life to encourage you or kick you in the pants when you need to keep going?

- If you don't have that person, what is your plan to get someone like that in your life?

Additional Study Verses

- Job 13:15
- Proverbs 24:16
- Acts 9:16
- Romans 5:3
- 1 Corinthians 4:12; 10:13
- 2 Corinthians 1:9
- Galatians 6:9
- Ephesians 6:18

- Philippians 1:12; 3:14
- 2 Timothy 2:3–4; 3:10–12
- Hebrews 12:3
- James 1:2–4, 12, 25
- 1 Peter 4:14–16
- 2 Peter 1:6
- Revelation 3:10

POWER:
THE HOLY SPIRIT UNLEASHED

The cross exists because we have failed.
—ANONYMOUS

God opens doors ...
but it is your job to walk through them.
—JOE PELLEGRINO

The Same Power that Raised Jesus from the Dead

When you are born again, God gives you the Holy Spirit to come and live inside of you. This is the same Holy Spirit who raised Jesus Christ from the dead and who raises you from being spiritually dead to becoming spiritually alive. And it is the same Holy Spirit who gives you the power to follow Jesus each and every day of your life. First Corinthians 4:20 says, "For the kingdom of God is not a matter of talk but of power." This is a man's Scripture if there ever was one! Let's take a closer look at what it means.

First, we have to realize that God is a King, and He rules His kingdom. In God's kingdom, He is in charge. He has dominion. What He says goes. When we choose to follow Jesus, we leave our little kingdom where we tried unsuccessfully to control everything, and we enter into His kingdom, where He reigns supreme.

When we rely on our own strength, we become limited by our weakness. But God is omnipotent, which means He is all powerful. Choosing to follow Jesus means giving up control of our lives and relying upon Jesus to be the power source in our day-to-day life. We need to stop using our own limited strength and abilities to follow Jesus, and instead we need to choose to follow Him in our thoughts, actions, and decisions. We have access to His unlimited power through the Holy Spirit. Let's use it.

When we choose to follow Jesus, the Holy Spirit comes and dwells within us. Again, this is the same Holy Spirit who raised Jesus Christ from the dead. Paul said in Romans 8:11, "And if the Spirit of him who raised Jesus from the dead is living in you, he who raised Christ from the dead will also give life to your mortal bodies because of his Spirit, who lives in you." This goes way beyond a guy who is dragged to church by his wife on Sunday morning. It's about the raw power of God living in us and working through us.

The Purpose of Power

There is something in men that loves power. We jump when we see a crushing home run, a monster dunk, or a knockout punch. We are wired for power. Following Christ is not about going to church and passively listening and forgetting what we heard.

When we go to church, we go because we want to learn how to walk in the power of the almighty God. Christ doesn't just want to modify our behavior; He wants to revolutionize our lives.

God gives us power to achieve His purposes. Those purposes include building strong marriages, conquering sinful habits, and being great fathers for our kids. What would your life look like if you functioned in more of God's power and less in your limitations? For far too long, men have spent their lives living in the power of the flesh instead of the power of the Holy Spirit.

The Generator

I (Joe) mentioned that in 2011 our house flooded from Hurricane Irene. In 2012, Hurricane Sandy hit, and we faced the threat of even more flooding. However, something almost worse than flooding happened—the power went out for seven solid days. How do you survive with no electricity for an entire week? Fortunately, we were blessed to have a generator. Unfortunately, when I tried to start the generator, it wouldn't start.

I kept trying to start the generator, but it just wouldn't turn over. I went through all the connections and they all seemed good. Since we had never actually used the generator before, I thought I might be overlooking something. So I asked a neighbor who is mechanically inclined to take a look at it. He came over, flipped the switch, pulled the cord, and it started right up. I was dumbfounded. I asked him what happened, and he told me, "You never engaged it. You had the fuse set to off." Many times, when we want to plug into power, we fail to engage; we fail to connect in a way that turns the power on.

I had a generator capable of powering my entire house, but it was not functioning. Similarly, many men have faith in Jesus as their Savior, but His strength is not running their lives. The connection is not being made with the Holy Spirit. Sin or unbelief is short-circuiting their connection to the power of the Holy Spirit in their day-to-day lives. They are not allowing Him to direct and empower every aspect of their lives, which means there is no power. My problem was not in the generator, but in the connection.

There is a great difference between calling Jesus our Savior and calling Him our Lord. A Lord controls you, and you yield to his wishes and hand him the keys to your life. This is a tough thing for men to do, but if we could fully understand the power that this generates, then watch out.

Breaking the Chains

One of the reasons we work so hard at Legacy Minded Men is because so many men are held in the chains of sin. Some men don't care because they love their sin, at least for a season. But at some point, many realize that the very thing that they would have called freedom and fun has sunk its teeth deep into them. The very thing they once bragged about and enjoyed now owns them. And so over time they begin to hate it, and often they don't know how to get out of its grip.

So many men, including good family men and even surprisingly many church leaders, including pastors, have become entangled in ongoing sin, such as pornography. Others are held in the chains of alcohol, drugs, and all kinds of sexual sins. Some are looking for the next thrill, while many others use their sin to medicate themselves from the pain of life.

When you come to Christ, the Holy Spirit gives you the power to break these sins. Just think if the Holy Spirit was powerful enough to raise Jesus from the dead after three days, then He certainly is powerful enough to break *any and every* habit or sin you have. Legacy Minded Men has an ongoing ministry called Breaking the Chains. This is a conference call where men can call in and hear from other men who have experienced the power of the Holy Spirit breaking patterns of sin and sexual addictions from their own lives. Many of these men struggled for years, some even for decades, but thanks to the power of the Holy Spirit they found freedom.

Pretty Good at Drinking Beer

Not only is "Pretty Good at Drinking Beer" a country song, but for too many men it is also their favorite hobby. It was mine (Jack's), and I was sure good at it. I began drinking on a regular basis when I was a freshman in high school. My friends and I got our start sneaking liquor from our parents' liquor cabinets. We would hide it in shampoo bottles and drink it on the boardwalk at the Jersey Shore. Then we started drinking beer and just kept on going.

Unlike many, I was a successful drunk. By that I mean I managed to complete high school, earn an academic scholarship for college, and after my undergraduate degree, go on to Columbia University, where I completed three master's degrees in two years. I could close the bar three or four nights a week and still get up at eight the next morning for a class. It was a gift. It also allowed me to live a lie and perpetuate a self-destructive lifestyle. Along the way, I hurt a lot of people and left a highway of relational wreckage behind me.

One Sunday morning in the summer of 1997, I heard a preacher tell the story of Jesus and how He came to pay for my sins so that I could be forgiven. He said that I could actually know God and that He would give me a new beginning. This was the first time I had ever heard this good news. Church people call it the gospel. I wasn't interested in a bunch of religious stuff or joining a church, but I did want a new beginning. I needed to be forgiven for a whole lot, and I wanted to know God.

I asked Jesus to forgive me and to come into my heart. I asked Him to give me the strength to follow Him. I meant it, but I didn't really know what I had done. In that moment, I opened up my heart and the Holy Spirit came and dwelt in me. I began a new life. Church people call it being "born again." I was not only forgiven, but I was instantly set free. From that moment on, I have never had another drink. From my understanding, when you have been a heavy drinker for ten to twelve years, stopping overnight is impossible. But that's what happened to me. In a moment, the Holy Spirit made me a new person, bringing life to my dead soul. And He is able to do the same for you too.

You Can't Handle the Truth

Okay … yes, it's an old movie line, but we love it. It highlights an important truth for us as Christians: we can't handle all the truth at one time. In fact, Jack Nicholson actually stole that line from Jesus. In John 16:12–13, Jesus says, "I still have many things to say to you, but you cannot bear them now. However, when He, the Spirit of truth, has come, He will guide you into all truth" (NKJV).

There have been times when we know that God or people were telling us the truth about things, but we either didn't know how to make the changes or just didn't want to (yet). But the Holy Spirit living within us keeps working on us until we are ready to make the change He desires. We can reject the truth and, in turn, reject God's power; however, that's not God's will for us, and it is a surefire recipe for a lousy legacy.

God is patient with us, but we can definitely speed up the

changes and release His power in our lives by allowing God to guide us. We leave too many things on the table when it comes to God. We need to stop doing that. Our kids, our wives, and the world need us to be walking in His power.

The 364-Day-Old Check

Back in 1989 when I (Joe) left my job to start my own business, it was lean times indeed. It was difficult as we tried to make a business work. I didn't know that much about starting a business, even though I had learned how to run one in my previous years. It was an interesting time and, like I said, it was lean.

We were struggling to pay our mortgage each month. In order to make the little money we had go even further, I decided to refinance our mortgage. In this process we had a month where we had no money and didn't have a clue how we were going to pay the mortgage. One day I received a call from my attorney. He told me that he needed the deed to my house. I had no idea where it might be, so I asked him where I would find it. He told me it would probably be with other papers from my last closing, which I had done the previous year.

I keep all my important papers in the family safe. So I unlocked the safe and began searching through the papers. I found an unopened letter from the attorney who handled my last closing. I opened the letter and, sure enough, there was the deed. I also started thumbing through the other papers in the enve-lope, and I came across something that was interesting. There was an uncashed refund check for almost the exact amount of my mortgage payment. I couldn't believe what I was seeing. I looked on the check and it was dated 364 days prior. One thing I had learned from my time in business was that banks will not cash a check that is more than 365 days old.

So I ran—and I mean *ran*—to the bank. I went to the drive-thru to deposit the check and the entire time I prayed, *Lord, let them say, "Have a good day."* Sure enough, the young lady came back and said, "Have a nice day!" The check went through, and I was able to make my mortgage payment.

I spent a lot of time praying and trying to understand how God was going to help me pay my mortgage. Then out of nowhere, God led me to a check I received 364 days earlier. The check had been waiting in the safe for almost a year. All I had to do was open up the safe and cash the check in order to have what I needed. Are you tapping into the power of the Holy Spirit to provide the power you need to live a legacy-minded life?

Just a Thought

How would your life look different if you were walking in God's power in greater ways? What is stopping you? Have you settled for being a Sunday morning Christian who doesn't read the Word or seek to live it out in your daily life? In what areas do you need to wave the white flag, surrender to Jesus, and ask for His power?

Get a coach. Nobody goes to the Olympics without a great coach. If those are physical races, then how much more important is a spiritual coach? Yes, this can be your pastor, but whom do you have on a regular, even daily, basis if needed, to coach you, encourage you, and help you walk in God's power?

Pillar Builders

- Read and study God's Word. It is important to know the truth, and the best way you can know the truth is to know God's Word.

- Have a daily quiet time. This is probably the most important thing you can do every day. During a daily quiet time take the time to pray, read God's Word, and focus on areas where you need to grow. There are many great books and resources to help you, which can also point you to specific Scriptures to focus on and live by.

- Focus on growing and not just trying to stop certain behaviors. The Holy Spirit empowers you when you walk in obedience to the Word and His leading. The more time you spend with God and following His leading, the more you will walk in His power.

Additional Study Verses

- Psalm 62:11
- Zechariah 4:6
- Matthew 6:13
- Mark 5:30
- Luke 24:49
- John 14:26; 16:12–13
- Acts 1:8; 4:33
- Romans 8:11, 31; 10:9
- 1 Corinthians 1:17; 2:4; 3:16; 4:20
- Ephesians 6:10
- Colossians 1:29
- 1 Thessalonians 1:5

NOW WHAT?

Process. Hey, maybe this is the next pillar? Just as salvation is the starting line, not the finish line, so your choice to become a legacy-minded man is *not* the finish line. Rather, it is only the beginning of an amazing spiritual journey. The truth is that you became who you are today because of a process—a process called "life"—and you are where you are because of the life process you have lived.

Not a New Year's Resolution

Becoming a legacy-minded man is not like the average New Year's resolution that lasts a week or two at best. It's not simply a decision to be forgiven by God, and then go on with life like you always have. It's a decision to become a God-empowered man whose life is something that can be proudly passed on to his children, both natural and spiritual.

We give you one final illustration before we leave you. When my son Joey was around eight, I (Joe) would take him in the backyard and teach him how to play baseball. The deal was that if he hit the ball over my head, I would buy him a big LEGO pirate ship, which he really wanted. Unfortunately, he never hit the ball over my head. Or did he?

My son thought he did. But I disagreed. Regardless, it obviously bothered him because he thought that I reneged on the deal. When Joey was twenty-four years old, he took a job in the Orlando area. In November 2013 we drove from New Jersey to Jacksonville, Florida, in record time. During our time in the car we had several conversations, mostly good. But there were a few that told me there still existed some tension between us.

Once we arrived, we needed to get him settled in his new apartment, so our first stop was at the local Walmart. As we shopped for cleaning supplies and various odds and ends, I came across the LEGO aisle. As I stood in front of the new version of the LEGO pirate ship, I realized that ship was creating a wedge between us, so I decided it was time I did something about it. When I flew home the very next day, my first stop was Walmart, where I purchased that pirate ship, wrapped it up, and waited for Christmas.

When Joey came home for Christmas, I could not wait to give him this special gift. After all the gifts were given out, I told Joey I had one more for him, but before he opened it he needed to first read the card I had written for him. It said simply:

Joey,
This is long overdue, and for that I am sorry. Please accept this, late as it may be, for the continual home runs you are hitting in your life.
—Love, Dad

The look on his face told the story. After reading the note, he said he knew exactly what the gift was. That day we spent Christmas at my brother-in-law Timmy's house. When Timmy asked Joey what he got for Christmas, Joey put his arm around me and said, "My dad never has to buy me another gift." That meant the world to me.

No matter how bad you screw up, no matter how many years have passed, you can always do something about your past mistakes. Even if the person you go back to fails to forgive you, you will be released. I am so thankful I tried to right a wrong, and I believe Joey and I are better for it. It's never too late to right a wrong done in the past.

If you want to be a legacy-minded man, it all begins with the right foundation. Jesus is the Rock on which we build our entire lives, the only real, solid foundation that stays dependable no matter what. Once we have that settled in our hearts and minds, then and only then can we start building on the seven pillars of a legacy-minded man.

A legacy-minded man is more concerned with becoming something than he is about checking off a to-do list. He is focused on understanding, not just some intellectual exercise. A legacy-minded man lives in two places at the same time. He gets up each day and fights to win the battle in front of him, but he also gazes into the future and lives in a manner that will build a lasting legacy.

God created you to win. So always remember that you are not in this alone. God is on your side, and so is an army of legacy-minded men. Jesus is the foundation, God's grace is the cement, and the Holy Spirit is the builder within those who rest in Christ's peace. Now that is a team we want to be a part of. How about you?

The Final Word

Life is funny. I (Joe) often laugh that God has chosen me to speak to men on many of the issues listed in this book. This can be especially humbling because everything I am encouraging you to do, I got wrong at some point in my life. I'm not expecting you to be perfect, and neither is God. This, of course, is no excuse to purposely and repetitively do wrong things. The reality is in my best efforts I still come up short at times. As a matter of fact, I still have difficulty dealing with things I have done. I know I cannot live in the past, nor can I change it—I can only learn from it.

I want to encourage you that, when you are not perfect, God gives grace. Grace does two things: it covers our mistakes and it also empowers us to do better the next time around. You can't do these things in your own strength—no one can—but you can do all things through Christ who gives you strength (Philippians 4:13). I get better because I refuse to quit and I refuse to settle. I believe you are a fighter too, whom God created to do amazing things. In fact, one of my favorite Scriptures captures it best: "Do you not know that in a race all the runners run, but only one gets the prize? Run in such a way as to get the prize" (1 Corinthians 9:24).

Transformed: The 7 Pillars of a Legacy Minded Man has laid out a winning game plan for your life. It is also important to remember that you are not in this alone: You have Jesus, and you have your church, and the larger body of Christ. Lastly, Legacy Minded Men is here for you and your church. We need each other to keep growing and to keep going. We can't wait to see and hear about the legacy God builds through your life. Please go to www.transformedtoday.com to tell us your story.

Now get out there and win!

ADDITIONAL RESOURCES

Legacy Minded Men

To host a Transformed conference or to find discipleship and groups tools, workshops, and much more, go to www.legacy mindedmen.org. You can also keep up with Legacy Minded Men on

Twitter: @legacymindedmen
Facebook: Legacy Minded Men -
   https://www.facebook.com/LLMNJ

Jack Redmond Ministries

Jack Redmond Ministries is a great resource for leadership training, church growth, regional conferences, youth ministry, blogs, books, podcasts, and more with Jack Redmond. For more information or to access these resources, go to

www.jackredmond.org.
Twitter: @jackwredmond
Facebook: Jack Redmond - https://www.facebook.com
   /Jack-Redmond-122638984452433/

ABOUT LEGACY MINDED MEN

www.LegacyMindedMen.org

Our Mission

Transforming lives by engaging, encouraging, and equipping men to build a Christ-centered legacy.

Our Vision

The vision of Legacy Minded Men is to move men from being unengaged and apathetic in their faith to men who are fully engaged and men of action. Through our servant-based ministry we come alongside the local church, both small and large, to help build or assist with their men's ministry, which, if done properly, will not only impact the church but the man himself. This in turn will affect his family, his workplace, and ultimately the community he serves in a powerful way.

Resources

Listed below are ten proven tools to launch, rebuild, or augment an existing men's ministry. They provide step-by-step instructions on how to incorporate these into your current program.

Some can be implemented at no charge, while others can be scheduled. They are:

1. Tools:
   - Prayer Call
   - Legacy Groups
   - Fathers Say
   - Mentoring 2 Maturity
   - Legacy Minded Men app (Download it today!)

2. Conference and Workshops:
   - Conference in a Box
   - Transformed Conference
   - 7 Pillars of a Legacy Minded Man Workshop
   - Huddle Up Workshop
   - Standing in the Gap Workshop

We at Legacy Minded Men are committed to your success. Our website, www.LegacyMindedMen.org, has a tremendous amount of resources to help any man, group, or church. Of course, you can always reach out to us via the website or by calling us at 973-865-8000. We hope you enjoy the journey.

ESTABLISHING AND SUSTAINING A STRONG LEGACY GROUP

Another great event. Men were moved. Excitement was generated. Now what? Too often this is where the ball stops rolling. But what if there was something on the back end that extended the life of the event? What if there was something that takes what the men learned and allows them to live it out? Maybe there was no event, but you just feel led to encourage and equip men to be all God created them to be. No matter the reason, Legacy Groups take men to a whole other level.

What Is a Legacy Group?

Legacy Groups are a unique tool that allow men the freedom to be real with each other. This fosters authentic relationships that encourage men to respond to the call of God. Legacy Groups are not for Bible study per se, although the Word of God is discussed. Rather, they are a place where men can be themselves and not worry about being judged. Truth spoken in love is a formula for transformation.

What's the Purpose of a Legacy Group?

These groups are designed to transform lives by engaging, encouraging, and equipping men to build a Christ-centered legacy.

Who Should Facilitate?

Not everyone is meant to facilitate a Legacy Group. The ideal candidate should be a man who is not shy and can keep the discussion going, which is extremely important to keep men engaged. He should also not be a people pleaser who tells the men what they want to hear or allows an unproductive discussion to continue. The entire meeting schedule will be sent via e-mail to the facilitator, so he only needs to take a few minutes to review the material prior to the meeting and pray for guidance.

What is the Facilitator's Role?

Here are a few pointers for those who are facilitating a Legacy Group.

- Don't let any one man dominate the whole conversation. Let the men know that if someone is dominating the conversation, you will interject to include more men in the discussion.

- We suggest you have men complete a survey, which will allow you to gauge where men are at in their life and walk. You can request the survey via the LMM website.

- Encourage the men to identify a man to be accountable to. Below are some recommended questions the men can ask each other:
  1. How are you doing with God?
  2. How are you doing with your spouse or the person you're dating?
  3. How are you doing with your children?

4. What temptations are you facing, and how are you dealing with them?
5. How has your thought life been this week?
6. Are you consistently living for Christ in your workplace?
7. Have you been spending regular time in the Word and in prayer?
8. With whom have you been sharing the gospel?
9. Have you lied in your answers to any of the questions above?
10. How may I pray for you and help you?

What Are the Groups Like?

Legacy Groups are ideally for two to fifteen men. While this may seem like a small number, it is essential in order to ensure the men feel comfortable and secure. It is also important to make men aware that the private information exchanged in the meeting should not be shared with anyone outside the group. If groups grow to more than fifteen, then we strongly suggest you identify a leader from the group and spin off a new group.

When and Where Should the Group Meet?

While there is no day or time better than any other, it is important to be consistent in your meeting times. For example, every Monday from 7:00–9:00 p.m., or every other Tuesday morning from 7:00–8:30 a.m. This will allow men to build it easily into their schedule. If you are catering to men who can't get together during the week, then you can schedule a Saturday meeting. The bottom line is to establish a time that works for those in the group.

Legacy Groups can be held at a church, a home, or even a local diner or coffee shop. Men can simply get together with a few friends, or it can be part of a church program. The important thing is that men meet together and be real and authentic in their relationships with one another.

What Are the Legacy Minutes?

Each week the facilitator will receive an e-mail from The Legacy Minute. This e-mail will provide a link to the weekly video topic and have a link to download the facilitator discussion questions.

How Are the Meetings Structured?

Each meeting should begin in the same manner:

1. Open in prayer.

2. Have men who are there for the first time introduce themselves.

3. Read the following to the group, at least for the first time (if you have the same group every time you meet, then it is fine to choose not to read it again):

   a. It is important to understand that you will be responsible to keep the discussion moving. Therefore, you will be limited to speak for no more than five minutes at one time. This will prevent any one person from dominating the conversation and allow for more men to chime in.

   b. Please be respectful of others' beliefs and their backgrounds.

   c. What is said in the group stays in the group. This is essential to build and maintain trust between attendees.

4. If a topic was discussed in the previous meeting where follow-up was requested, then address feedback at this time.

5. Play the weekly two- to five-minute video.

6. Use the video companion questions. If the group gets off on a tangent, allow it as long as it is constructive. Just make sure you eventually get them back on course.

7. Discuss any projects or activities the group may be interested in engaging together.

8. Take prayer requests.

9. Close in prayer.

If you wish to take a different approach, you certainly may. For example, if you want to have your group meet one week and then the following week have the group get together to help someone do a project, that would be great. You may also want to skip the video and go directly to the discussion questions. If you want men to go through a series, such as *Wild at Heart*, by John Eldredge, or *Stepping Up*, by Dennis Rainey, that would work well too.

Why Is It Important to Upload Meeting Notes?

So we may track the progress of your group, we ask that you log onto our website and answer a few simple questions, including the number of men who attended. The update will take no more than one minute.

What Are the Benefits of a Legacy Group?

- Unlike the average church men's ministry, Legacy Groups deal with issues that are all too real for men.

- Legacy Groups promote the building of strong relationships with an emphasis on accountability.

- By establishing a Legacy Group at your church, you plug into the LMM network, which will enable your men to participate in large regional conferences and workshops.

- Men will engage with other men of different backgrounds and cultures, breaking down barriers that exist in the church and society as a whole.

- Every two weeks Legacy Group leaders will receive an e-mail from LMM, which will feature a brief instructional video as well as a PDF to provide them with some talking points and solid discussion questions that they will facilitate.

What Are People Saying about Legacy Groups?

Establishing a Legacy Group was better than I could have imagined, thank you so so much, we are really indebted.

—PASTOR CHRIS LAWRENCE, CHURCH OF THE LIVING HOPE

Every time we get together, we grow with one another more. This includes doing activities together that months ago we never would've done. In fact, today, ten of us (of varying ages) were playing baseball together in the church yard! And tomorrow, we are going to play baseball at a much larger field. As always, God is glorified.

—PASTOR ERNESTO MARIN, HAVANA, CUBA

We are indeed indebted to you.

—Pastor Adonai Magwaza, Zimbabwe, Africa

LMM Partners is such an asset to the body of Christ. It builds the regional church while strengthening the local church.

—Pastor Peter Bruno, Metro Church

What If I Still Have Questions?

If you have any questions, please visit www.LegacyMindedMen. org. We are here to help.

LEGACY MINUTES

FOURTEEN-WEEK
LEGACY GROUP DISCUSSION STARTERS

Week 1

Pillar 1: Prayer

Just a Thought: Prayer invites God into your situation so that you have God's strength and wisdom involved in overcoming or solving a problem.

Scripture: "You do not have, because you do not ask God" (James 4:2).

Discussion Questions:

1. What does it mean that prayer is simply "talking to God"?

2. What areas in your life have you tried to change but not seen the change you desire?

3. How could answered prayer change your life now?

4. Have you made a list of things to consistently pray about until God gives you the strategy, strength, or provision you need to turn situations around?

5. How could answered prayer change your legacy?

6. Who are the people around you, and what are the situations at work or in society that need your prayers?

Legacy Lifter: Whom do you have in your life who needs your physical help and prayers? Start to make a list of people you can help, serve, and pray for. It may be wise to focus on helping only one or two at a time, depending on the situation. Watch what God will do as you help them win, both spiritually and naturally.

Week 2

Pillar 2: Persona

Just a Thought: Persona is who you are at your core and in the toughest times of your life. It is often shaped and defined by those you surround yourself with and listen to.

Scripture: "There is a way that seems right to a man, but its end is the way of death" (Proverbs 14:12 NKJV).

Discussion Questions:

1. Who do you really think you are at your core?

2. Do the people around you encourage you to be your best or pull you away from your destiny and legacy?

3. Whom do you have in your life that is building your persona and legacy?

4. What type of people do you need to add to your life to fully live out your purpose?

5. Are there any people you may need to limit or remove from your regular interactions?

6. Whom are you pouring your life into in order to build their persona and character?

Legacy Lifter: One of the key factors of building our legacy is first being built-up and strong ourselves. We often want to help others, but this is best done from a place of strength. Make a list of three areas you need to grow in, and then find one to three men to help you grow in these areas. This will help you build your persona. These types of relationships can speak wisdom into your life, because not everything that seems right at the moment is the right thing to do.

Week 3

Pillar 3: Purity

Just a Thought: Purity may not be a popular discussion at the ball game or in the boardroom, but it is a huge issue when it comes to connecting with God and walking in His power. Having a clean mind and heart is the foundation to having clean words and actions. Purposely engaging in impure and sinful activities basically tells God that those things are more important than He is. Purity opens the door to His presence and power, while purposeful impurity shuts that door.

Scripture: "Who may ascend the mountain of the LORD? Who may stand in his holy place? The one who has clean hands and a pure heart, who does not trust in an idol or swear by a false god" (Psalm 24:3–4).

Discussion Questions:

1. Have you ever thought that by choosing to focus on or engage in impure thoughts and actions, you are telling God you don't want Him?

2. What's the difference between having an impure thought and purposely focusing on or living in that thought or lifestyle?

3. Have you ever thought that when a person chooses impurity, they not only lose God, but God loses them too?

4. Have you ever been mad at God for not helping you, but now realize that you chose something else over His help?

5. How has society made impurity seem normal?

6. Has this discussion stirred you to make some changes?

Legacy Lifter: Purity, or the lack of it, is handed down from generation to generation. In addition, we live in a generation that is promoting impurity more than any other in history. You can make changes to ensure you are passing along a pure legacy to your children and grandchildren. It is also important to help young men navigate such an impure world. Is there another man whom you can have a purity discussion with? It would be great to help him take some action steps to establish and maintain a pure lifestyle.

Week 4

Pillar 4: Purpose

Just a Thought: Living out our life's purpose can be challenging at times. First, we have to discover what it is. And even when we know that, we have to then organize our life to live it out. The reality is that if you sat down with the average guy and asked him if he knew whether or not he was living out his life's purpose, you would probably get a blank stare and not much of a response. God clearly created us for a purpose, but we will never live it out without being intentional in its pursuit.

Scripture: "'For I know the plans I have for you,' declares the LORD, 'plans to prosper you and not to harm you, plans to give you hope and a future'" (Jeremiah 29:11).

Discussion Questions:

1. Do you feel like your life has a purpose?

2. Can you describe your life's purpose in one sentence?

3. What's the difference between being busy and living out your purpose?

4. What things do you need to do differently to live out your purpose?

5. What are some roadblocks that need to be removed to live out your purpose?

6. Whom do you have in your life to encourage and help you live out your purpose?

Legacy Lifter: Life's purpose comes from God giving us a vision (Proverbs 29:18), which causes us to order our lives in a way to actually live it out. Having vision and a plan to live out your purpose is the difference between living a great life or just sitting on a bar stool and talking about the glory days. The thing you feel as the greatest burden on your heart is most likely connected to your purpose. Spend time with God, dream, and then go for it.

Week 5

Pillar 5: Priorities

Just a Thought: We live in the busiest and most stressful time in the history of the world. We have never had so many things pulling at us and interrupting us. The danger of this is that all of these things eat away at our time and pull us away from our priorities. The key to living out our purpose is to establish our priorities and then live our life in a way that focuses on achieving them.

Scripture: "Put your outdoor work in order and get your fields ready; after that, build your house" (Proverbs 24:27).

Discussion Questions:

1. What are the three most important things in your life?

2. Are you living your life based on a set of priorities or just handling issue after issue as they come up?

3. Do you write down your priorities regularly and life goals annually?

4. Do you regularly schedule significant time to achieve your priorities?

5. What are some things you can minimize or eliminate in order to give you more time, energy, and resources to focus on your priorities?

6. Have you had significant and ongoing discussions with your spouse and/or family about establishing and living out your priorities?

Legacy Lifter: Writing down your priorities and then scheduling time to achieve them is a powerful tool. It is also a powerful legacy builder. You can also help others establish this powerful habit. Maybe you can identify a young man in your life who needs help writing out his priorities, thus helping him establish a life plan to achieve.

Week 6

Pillar 6: Perseverance

Just a Thought: Perseverance is the ability to stay focused and to keep going through all of life's trials and all of the things that pull you away from your priorities. Perseverance is also the conviction to keep going and never quit on your marriage, your faith, or your family. It learns from failure or inability, and it drives you to keep growing.

Scripture: "Let us not become weary in doing good, for at the proper time we will reap a harvest if we do not give up" (Galatians 6:9).

Discussion Questions:

1. On a scale from 1 to 10—1 being "I'm a big-time quitter" and 10 being "I'll die before I quit"—who are you at your core?

2. What are two or three things you are committed to persevering in?

3. Have you written down the steps you need to take in order to achieve your desired goals and life outcomes?

4. Do you have a lifestyle that includes things like exercise, rest, daily quiet time with the Lord, and other disciplines to keep you strong and help you not become weary?

5. What are some nonessentials, which are using up your time and energy, you could eliminate from your life?

6. Have you established people in your life who encourage you to persevere and hold you up when you feel weary?

Legacy Lifter: George Patton said, "Fatigue makes cowards of us all."[11] We have to look at weariness as an enemy that will make us cowards, not able to persevere. Many men are too tired to fight for their marriages and families, and many men fall into sin when weary. We often give our wife and children leftovers because we spent all of our energy at work or elsewhere. So we must choose daily to set our priorities straight and then give our best every day and never quit. Perseverance is a daily choice to demand that we live out God's best in our lives.

Week 7

Pillar 7: Power

Just a Thought: The *kingdom of God* is a phrase that describes how God rules and works in His authority and power. When we choose to follow Christ, we choose to live in His kingdom—His domain. This opens us up to God's power working in us and through us.

Scripture: "For the kingdom of God is not a matter of talk but of power" (1 Corinthians 4:20).

Discussion Questions:

1. On a scale from 1 to 10, how much are you working in your own strength? How much is in God's strength?

2. What are some areas where you have tried to change but need God's strength and power to really change?

3. How much time do you daily spend reading God's Word and praying?

4. Who are some spiritually powerful people you spend time with?

5. When was the last time you found a Scripture that addressed a life issue, and you memorized or stood on that Scripture until God changed the situation?

6. What adjustments can you make in your life in order to walk in more of God's power?

Legacy Lifter: The reason many men don't like going to church is because it is often a passive exercise of sitting and listening. Men don't want to sit; they want to do. If you have settled for religious activity, you can go deeper, build your faith, and walk in God's power in greater ways. Identify an issue and don't settle for the status quo, but have faith and work to win that battle or overcome that obstacle.

Week 8

Pillar 1: Prayer

Just a Thought: God created us for His pleasure, and He desires a best friend relationship with each and every one of us. Our time with Him brings together pieces, parts, ideas, and opportunities in order to be successful.

Scripture: "And without faith it is impossible to please God, because anyone who comes to him must believe that he exists and that he rewards those who earnestly seek him" (Hebrews 11:6).

Discussion Questions:

1. What pleasure does God get from us praying?

2. In our hectic lives, what practical ways can we spend time with Him?

3. What rewards come from prayer?

4. Prayer is more than one person talking; what other piece(s) can be a part of prayer?

5. You make the time for things you have placed as a priority in your life. Prayer is on your list, but what priority have you actually made it?

6. Why do we say "prayer changes things"?

Legacy Lifter: If prayer is both parties talking, then it would be a great idea to bring a pad and paper with you when you pray. God loves giving you thoughts, images, and Scriptures that will lift you, inspire you, and answer the very requests that you have asked of Him.

Week 9

Pillar 2: Persona

Just a Thought: When God walked into your life, His DNA began connecting to your DNA. His life is now growing ever stronger within you.

Scripture: "He must increase, but I must decrease" (John 3:30).

Discussion Questions:

1. How has your persona changed since you started a relationship with Christ?

2. Can you sense areas that may not have changed yet, but you can tell Jesus is hard at work on them? What are some of those areas?

3. If Christ lives within you, what are practical ways you can become more like Him?

4. What are ways you can allow His grace (compassion, favor, forgiveness, kindness, goodness, and love) to shine through you?

5. What people have noticed (or been affected) by your persona since you met Jesus?

Legacy Lifter: The kingdom of darkness is not afraid of Jesus in you; rather, it is afraid of Jesus coming out of you. So you can "let Him out" more often.

Week 10

Pillar 3: Purity

Just a Thought: God's desire is to raise us up to His level by giving us His standard for our life.

Scripture: "Therefore, if anyone is in Christ, he is a new creation; the old has gone, the new has come!" (2 Corinthians 5:17).

Discussion Questions:

1. Purity is God's moving-in system—He moves His furniture in and He moves your things out. What item(s) is God rearranging on the inside of you?

2. You no doubt have experienced changes of purity within you. How has your family, marriage, and kids reacted to it?

3. Sometimes we can wrestle with our desires versus God's desires. What struggles have you had when wrestling with the issue of desires?

Legacy Lifter: God's desire is to continue to make you, mold you, and disciple you to become more and more like Jesus. The more you yield to the Holy Spirit, the greater the changes taking place within you.

Week 11

Pillar 4: Purpose

Just a Thought: Your path and destiny upon the earth are wrapped in two words: divine purpose. You are not an accident, an afterthought, or a mistake. You are part of God's plan, having been thought of and chosen from before the foundation of the world.

Scripture: "And we know that in all things God works for the good of those who love him, who have been called according to his purpose" (Romans 8:28).

Discussion Questions:

1. Divine purpose has tools. What gifts, talents, and dreams do you have?

2. Divine purpose is valuable—it needs to be protected at all times. Have you had any struggles with who people said you were or weren't?

3. Have you ever experienced lost hope, a lack of purpose, or a loss of earthly direction? Explain.

Legacy Lifter: When you turn your life toward God's purpose, your dreams, goals, and desires come alive. You begin to see how important you are in God's eyes.

Week 12

Pillar 5: Priority

Just a Thought: Priorities are the foundations that your house of life will be built upon. They become life goals that help set your path and direction.

Scripture: "But everyone who hears these words of mine and does not put them into practice is like a foolish man who built his house on sand" (Matthew 7:26).

Discussion Questions:

1. Priorities. We all have them. What are your top five priorities?

2. God loves replacing our priorities with His. Are there a couple of priorities in your life that you'd like God to swap out?

3. What are practical ways you can make your marriage a priority? How about your kids? How about your relationship with God?

4. How does your career fit into your list of priorities?

Legacy Lifter: If you haven't made a list of priorities yet, begin to pray and start writing them down. A great idea is to have a pastor or church leader review your list, allowing him to comment on it, helping you define what is really important. Where your priorities are, there time and finances will follow.

Week 13

Pillar 6: Perseverance

Just a Thought: Perseverance will see you through. Many times the first impulse is to quit and succumb, but perseverance gets you to the other side of that difficulty.

Scripture: "Therefore, among God's churches we boast about your perseverance and faith in all the persecutions and trials you are enduring" (2 Thessalonians 1:4).

Discussion Questions:

1. Have you ever quit anything that you still regret? Explain.

2. Are there things now you're tempted to give up on? If so, what?

3. Not giving up sounds great, but what are some practical steps to keep going?

Legacy Lifter: Nonenduring tools fail under pressure. God has formed you as a tool He can use in difficult situations that will get the job done and bless others. The choice to continue is yours!

Week 14

Pillar 7: Power

Just a Thought: Power is summed up easily in the person of the Holy Spirit. The key to our victory is to rely on Him for everything.

Scripture: "But you will receive power when the Holy Spirit comes on you; and you will be my witnesses in Jerusalem, and in all Judea and Samaria, and to the ends of the earth" (Acts 1:8).

Discussion Questions:

1. God is still a God of power. What miracles have you seen?

2. God is love, so His power works toward people. What practical ways can you release His compassion toward people who are hurting?

3. What are ways you can depend on the Holy Spirit more in your daily life?

Legacy Lifter: When your strength is gone or feels weak, that's when God's strength takes over.

To receive a new lesson each week, download the Legacy Minded Men App or view all the Legacy Minutes at www.LegacyMindedMen.org under Resources.

ABOUT THE AUTHORS

Joe Pellegrino is an author, speaker, publisher, certified life coach, consultant, and entrepreneur. He is also the president and founder of Legacy Minded Men, whose mission is to "transform lives by engaging, encouraging, and equipping men to build a Christ-centered legacy." Joe is the coauthor of the books *Safe at Home* and *That's My Dad!* Joe has also developed and presents several workshops and seminars, including "Standing in the Gap," "Not Just an Average Joe," and "Transformed." He and his wife, Bethanne, have three children and reside in Wayne, New Jersey. To learn more about Joe, go to www.joepellegrino.com.

Other Books by Joe Pellegrino

Safe at Home (Chicago: Moody Press, 1993)

That's My Dad! (Racine, WI: BroadStreet Publishing Group, 2016)

Jack Redmond is an author, speaker, certified life coach, and church growth consultant. He is also the Church Mobilization Pastor at Christ Church, an eight-thousand-member church located in New Jersey. He is a sought-after speaker for conferences, leadership development, and church growth training. He has authored or coauthored six books. He and his wife, Antoinette, live in New Jersey with their four children. To connect with Jack, go to www.jackredmond.org.

Other Books by Jack Redmond

Let Your Voice Be Heard: Transforming from Church Goer to Active Soul Winner (New York: Morgan James Publishing, 2016)

God Belongs in My City, in partnership with Urban Kingdom Youth Ministries and www.Godbelongsinmycity.com (2011)

Infusion: Receive. Grow. Give it Away... (Alachua, FL: Bridge Logos, 2010)

Wounded Heart: Keys to Overcoming Life's Pain and Disappointment (Maitland, FL: Xulon Press, 2009)

People Matter to God: Experiencing Personal Transformation and Sharing It with Others (Maitland, FL: Xulon Press, 2008)

HOST A TRANSFORMED CONFERENCE OR WORKSHOP!

Go to
www.TransformedToday.com
for more information

ENDNOTES

1 "Legacy," Dictionary.com, unabridged (Random House, Inc.), http://www.dictionary.com/browse/legacy.

2 J. Oswald Sanders, *Spiritual Leadership* (Chicago: Moody Press, 1994).

3 John C. Maxwell, *The 21 Irrefutable Laws of Leadership: Follow Them and People Will Follow You* (Nashville, TN: Thomas Nelson Publishers, 1998), 110.

4 "Responsible Fatherhood," US Department of Justice Center for Faith Based & Neighborhood Partnerships, http://ojp.gov/fbnp/fatherhood.htm.

5 Samuel Ha, "Top 30 Greatest Mike Tyson Quotes," Mighty Fighter, http://www.mightyfighter.com/top-30-greatest-mike-tyson-quotes/.

6 Mike Tyson, "My Life As a Young Thug," *New York Magazine*, http://nymag.com/news/features/mike-tyson-2013-10/index1.html.

7 Ibid.

8 Ibid.

9 Les Brown, Goodreads, https://www.goodreads.com/quotes/884712-the-graveyard-is-the-richest-place-on-earth-because-it.

10 Charles E. Hummel, *Tyranny of the Urgent* (Downers Grove, IL: InterVarsity Press, 1994), 1.

11 George S. Patton Jr., *War as I Knew It*, as cited by Goodreads, http://www.goodreads.com/quotes/4281-fatigue-makes-cowards-of-us-all.

www.LegacyMindedMen.org